SPERM

CACHALOT
by
Jacques Miroir

adapted by
Tom Jacobson

BROADWAY PLAY PUBLISHING INC
224 E 62nd St, NY, NY 10065
www.broadwayplaypub.com
info@broadwayplaypub.com

First printing: June 2014
I S B N: 978-0-88145-599-1

Book design: Marie Donovan
Page make-up: Adobe Indesign
Typeface: Palatino
Printed and bound in the U S A

PUBLISHED BY B P P I

THE BELOVED DISCIPLE

BUNBURY

THE CHINESE MASSACRE (ANNOTATED)

EAT THE RUNT *(written as Avery Crozier)*

THE FRIENDLY HOUR

HOUSE OF THE RISING SON

TAINTED BLOOD

OUROBOROS

THE TWENTIETH-CENTURY WAY

SPERM was first produced by Circle X Theatre Company (Stan Weightman Jr, Producer; Josh Costello, Melanie Hermann & Valerie Gordon, Associate Producers) at 24th Street Theatre, running from 4 March-17 April 2004. The cast and creative contributors were:

RICHARD...Joel McHale
LOUIS XVI ....Jim Anzide
MARIE ANTOINETTE ....Michaela Watkins
DUC DE COIGNY...Casey Smith
SISTER LOUISE ....Sarah Hartmann
SEAMAN...D P Wichert
SEAMAN.. Thomas Fiscella
SEAMAN..Matt Ford
BARMAID ....Jen Kays
SEAMAN...David Holmes

Understudies.....Julie Alexander, Jen Kays, Jacob Sidney, Thia Stephan

Co-Director .... Tara Flynn
Co-Director ....Tim Wright
Assistant director.....................................Holly Gabrielson
Set designer/FX.....................................Richard Augustine
Lighting designer...Jonathan Klein
Sound designer/composer .... Tim Labor
Costume designer...Cynthia Herteg
Properties designer..Ali Hisserich
Scenic artist/floor design...................................Katia Kaplan
Fight choreography ....David Holmes
Fight choreography .... D P Wichert

CHARACTERS & SETTING

seven actors:

RICHARD, *20s, an American whaler*
LOUIS XVI, *30s, King of France*
MARIE ANTOINETTE, *30s, Queen of France*
DUC DE COIGNY, *20s-40s, First Equerry of Versailles, a nobleman*
SISTER LOUISE, *50s-70s, aunt of* LOUIS, *a Carmelite nun*
BARMAID

FRENCH AND ENGLISH SEAMEN, AMERICAN WHALERS, ACIDS, SERVANTS

Doubling may be as follows: SISTER LOUISE/BARMAID, FRENCH SEAMAN/AMERICAN WHALER/ACID/SERVANT, ENGLISH SEAMAN/AMERICAN WHALER/ACID/ SERVANT.

The action takes place in various locations in France from 1786 to 1789.

Locations are defined as simply as possible with furniture and lighting. When characters "swim", the actors are flown by wires or bungee cords.

ADAPTER'S NOTE

Jacques Miroir is almost certainly a pseudonym. Records show no noble of that name among the courtiers of Louis XVI, and a commoner would have no knowledge of the tragic intrigues and political machinations at court prior to the Revolution. The semi-Republican sympathies expressed in the play would have been unusual among the nobility, but the sympathetic portrayal of the royals would seem even more bizarre coming from the bourgeoisie. The peasantry had generally warm feelings for the King (if not the Queen), but few of them were literate during his reign. Who, then, wrote *Cachalot*?

It has been suggested that the true author is Beaumarchais, who may have decided to use a *nom de plume* in the wake of the outcry against *The Barber of Seville* and *The Marriage of Figaro*, plays that critique the nobility but without libeling living (royal!) persons. *Cachalot*, however, is in verse, unlike the work of Beaumarchais, and was probably considered stylistically archaic at the time. It resembles—although only superficially—the style of Molière. The content is almost Rabelaisian in scale. The sometimes scatological humor is most similar to the pornographic plays privately performed in 18th-century France.

The archaic style and the conflicting sympathies of *Cachalot* seem to have rendered it impossible to stage in the 1790s, for no record exists of even a private production. Royalists would have been horrified at its irreverence and improprieties, and the Jacobins would have shunned it as effete and *ancien* as the *regime* itself. Of course, the most probable reason the play was never produced lay in the author's extraordinary bad timing: who had time to produce a play when the best theatre was in the streets, complete with barricades, tumbrils, and guillotines—

No credence whatsoever should be given to the notion that the play was authored by Marie Antoinette during her imprisonment. The vulgarity of the language, not to mention the brutality of much of the action, indicates *Cachalot* could not have been written by a noblewoman of the 1790s, much less a queen!

ACT ONE

(A tavern in Dunkerque, 1786. Three SEAMEN *are drinking, occasionally served by a* BARMAID.*)*

FRENCH SEAMAN:
A whore's a whore, no matter where she lies.

ENGLISH SEAMAN:
Perhaps, my friend—and yet a whore who plies
Her trade on any shore betrays her birth
When quoting price.

FRENCH SEAMAN: Her nation is her worth—

ENGLISH SEAMAN:
Exactly, sir, so twat in France is free.

FRENCH SEAMAN:
I pay much more than that!

ENGLISH SEAMAN: It's quite a fee:
You pay with pox and chancres. Plus, she reeks
Of cloying perfume slathered on her cheeks.
All four, I mean, because she never wipes
Her arse, or bathes. A toast:
(Toasting)
                              The guttersnipes
Of France! The poon-tang of Paris! To Gaul!

FRENCH SEAMAN:
Monsieur, try as you might, I will not brawl
With any Englishman who eats our tarts
Then dares critique the recipe, and farts

Out clouds of lies. Your judgment must be weighed
Against the English way of getting laid.

ENGLISH SEAMAN:
I sense a rude remark—what's that you said?

FRENCH SEAMAN:
French harlots stink and steal but yours—are dead.

ENGLISH SEAMAN:
Perhaps my French is rusty—did you say
That English strumpets seem to pass away
From passion, swooning at *le petit morte?*

FRENCH SEAMAN:
They're morte before they start! I can report
From actual experience—they're dead!

ENGLISH SEAMAN:
You mean extinct?

FRENCH SEAMAN: I'll be succinct: in bed
An English lady of the night is cold
As marble and as soft to touch. An old,
Rank, rotting flounder makes a better fuck
And you can eat it after—no such luck
With girls in English ports. They won't do this,
They won't do that. You go to take a piss
Then when you're back they've gone straight off to
    sleep—
And stolen all the covers in a heap.
They snore like demons bellowing in pain.
I'll die before I bed a British whore again.

ENGLISH SEAMAN:
And so you shall, unless you take that back!

FRENCH SEAMAN:
I insult British bawds, then you attack!
Seems English dignity's a fragile thing.
I only hope for your sake that the Eng-

(Pulling out a knife)
-Lishmen brawl better than their women screw—

ENGLISH SEAMAN:
(Lunging with his knife.)
For God and England's whores, I'll run you through—!

RICHARD:
(The third SEAMAN, *bearded. Interposing)*
Boys! Boys!

FRENCH SEAMAN: You limey bastard!

ENGLISH SEAMAN: Slimy frog!

RICHARD:
(Keeping them at bay with his harpoon)
Don't slay yourselves like soldiers in a fog.
It's only Greeks and Trojans die for sluts!

ENGLISH SEAMAN:
I die for honor, sir!

FRENCH SOLDIER: For France!

RICHARD: You're nuts!
And drunk as rats in hogsheads!

FRENCH SOLDIER: So?

ENGLISH SOLDIER: So what?

RICHARD:
You don't got much to argue on, not squat!
The British tart, she has her faults, and yes,
French wenches sometimes offer even less.
But harlots from my country be the worst
The pussy from America—she cursed!

FRENCH SEAMAN:
(After staring for a moment)
Monsieur, you have just raped my mother tongue!

RICHARD:
Pardon my French. I learnt my words unstrung

When yellow fever made New Orleans my home
By keeping me in bed there all alone—
American amid the Spanish and the French.
My teachers were Delirium and Stench.

ENGLISH SEAMAN:
They get around! My French instructors were
The same!

FRENCH SEAMAN:
(Threatening again)
        Don't be so goddam fresh, Monsieur!

ENGLISH SEAMAN:
Relax! I want to hear why trollops of
The Colonies are bad at making love.

FRENCH SEAMAN:
Because they are descended from your race!

(Some commotion outside)

RICHARD:
It's commerce—how you say? The "marketplace".
They aim to please, above all else. They'll do
What wrings a coin or two more out of you.
They second guess, anticipate, and plan
Bizarre, exotic tanglings for their man.

ENGLISH SEAMAN:
It sounds like heaven!

FRENCH SEAMAN: Paradise!

RICHARD: It's not.
Their false enthusiasm selling cunt
Cannot arouse a man, but only blunt
His blade. They laugh when roughly stroked,
And counterfeit a shriek of joy when poked
As if it pleased them so to be with you
When, in fact, that night you're twenty-two
Of forty men she'll ball before the dawn.
I tell you, lads, it makes me want to yawn

Or get—oh, now what is the word—depressed
Each time a Yankee gets herself undressed,
Drops every stitch of clothes, but never strips
That sweet insipid smile from on her lips.
When all the while she's thinking that your prick
A-plunging deep inside her makes her sick.
You'd rather be despised by mademoiselles,
Ignored by corpse-like English Jezebels,
Than let a Yankee doodle with your toy.
Instead, jump back on ship and plug a boy.

(Increased hubbub outside. FRENCH SEAMAN *and* ENGLISH
SEAMAN *peer out the window.)*

ENGLISH SEAMAN:
What's all that row?

FRENCH SEAMAN: This is a quiet port
Most days.

RICHARD:
(Still seated)
               I'm sure it's only young lads making sport—

ENGLISH SEAMAN:
Oh, no, they're angry—brawling down the street.

FRENCH SEAMAN:
It's not just boys—it's merchants—

ENGLISH SEAMAN: Primed to beat
Somebody with those sticks—

(Hubbub dies down.)

FRENCH SEAMAN:
(Returning to the table)
                              Our bourgeoisie
Who hoard the grain, blame aristocracy
When peasants starve. Some poor, unlucky lord
Must be their prey.
(To RICHARD*)*

Are you so bored
You can't be stirred by revolution, boy—

RICHARD:
That mob of shopkeepers will just annoy
Your government. A revolution is
On grander scale. My noble father—his
Revolt created a new land.

ENGLISH SEAMAN: Do tell.

RICHARD:
A giant of a man, he did compel
Me to sit out the war—I was too young,
He said. Twas true, but even so, it stung.
Denied his path to glory, I set sail
Pursuing something grander yet—the whale.

FRENCH SEAMAN:
Monsieur, you mean you're on a whaling trip?

RICHARD:
We've only docked today—
(Pointing)
        —And there's my ship.

ENGLISH SEAMAN:
But there's no whaling out of France.

FRENCH SEAMAN:
We leave
That nasty task to Dutch and Englishmen to heave
Harpoons at monsters of the deep. Amer-
'Icans as well kill whales for they're
Barbarians from birth. But Frenchmen?

(Hubbub outside again)

RICHARD: —Sail
For whale but always seem—the word—to fail.
I've seen them get in boats to chase a wave,
Thinking it a fluke and themselves brave.
But your own king has given up on you

And asked Nantucket Islanders to do
The job of training France to hunt the fish
That lights the lamps, and so his wish
Is my com—com—

FRENCH SEAMAN: Command.

RICHARD: Command.

FRENCH SEAMAN: You've met
The King? I heard he's coming here.

*(The hubbub is louder, with discernable shouts and the
sound of carriage wheels.)*

RICHARD: Not yet.
I'm one of hundreds. Many families
Have started on their way across the seas
To colonize this paltry port with men
Who probe the mysteries of Leviathan.

*(The door flies open and three cloaked strangers burst in, led
by a woman, who is shouting. The clatter and other shouting
in the street is very loud.)*

WOMAN:
Turn out the Bourbons! Chase them down! Throw
                                                    rocks!

MAN: Don't shout like that!

WOMAN: The door!

MAN: And lock the locks!

*(The other MAN slams the door shut and locks it. The clatter
and hubbub quickly die away. The WOMAN peers out the
window.)*

WOMAN: The carriage lamp is broken, but they're gone.

MAN: How can you say those things?

WOMAN:
(To the SEAMEN as she goes to a different table)

                                          Please do go on.
Don't let us interrupt.

(The two MEN *smile nervously at the* SEAMEN, *then join the*
WOMAN *at her table.)*

FRENCH SEAMAN: It's just a tale
Of how to change the world by chasing whale.

ENGLISH SEAMAN:
Come bragging boy, can whaling men top this?
You'd whimper, cry, and douse your pants with piss
If you'd seen ghost ships on the Goodwin Sands—

FRENCH SEAMAN:
Or Flying Dutchman off of Afric lands—

RICHARD:
You've seen these haunts—

ENGLISH SEAMAN: The ghost ship? Oh, yes—
twice.

FRENCH SEAMAN:
The Flying Dutchman turned my blood to ice—

*(*FRENCH SEAMAN *pulls off his cap revealing a shock of pure*
white hair. Everyone gasps, including the eavesdroppers.)

FRENCH SEAMAN:
Then this I found upon my head. And yet—
Until that night it was as black as jet.

ENGLISH SEAMAN:
A charming anecdote, well told. Perhaps
A bit too perfectly rehearsed. Some chaps
Might say too good to be believed—

FRENCH SEAMAN:
(Pulling out his knife)   You dog—!

RICHARD:
(Intervening)
Now, boys, it's clear you've both had too much grog!
(To the ENGLISH SEAMAN*)*

A sly retort is always on your tongue—
(To the FRENCH SEAMAN*)*
Your knife is always out—you're highly strung.
Myself, I honor both your tales as true
Because I know a yarn that will outdo
You both.

ENGLISH SEAMAN: Let's hear it then.

FRENCH SEAMAN: Commence.

(Unable to stop himself, one of the eavesdroppers bursts out.)

LOUIS: Oh, please!

(The other eavesdroppers quickly restrain the embarrassed
LOUIS.*)*

RICHARD:
(Keenly aware of his expanded audience)
Again, forgive my French, before I seize
Upon this ghastly, ghostly legend I've
In mind. It's so grotesque you might derive
No pleasure from my recitation, but
It's morally instructive, not just smut.
(Throughout his tale, he carefully puts out the candles in the
room until only one remains.)

FRENCH SEAMAN:
A filthy phantom—better still!

RICHARD: The mate
Aboard my ship told me this story. Fate
Arranged his role the night this tale played out
Its horrifying, vengeful turnabout.
Have any of you been a-whaling?

ALL:
(Including the eavesdroppers)
                              No.

RICHARD:
Well, any man who gets a chance should go.

That's where this saga starts, upon the sea
Just as a right whale met its destiny.
They're named "right whales" because they are the
   ones
Who in their jaws grow what we call whalebones,
The stays in ladies' corsets made to press
Against the breasts and belly in a dress.
The chase was long and hazardous—
A bosun lost his arm—this succubus,
This creature, after fighting for her life
Rolled on her side, exhausted from the strife
And cast one rolling eye upon the mate.
He later said he'd never seen such hate
From any animal, not dog or horse.
The agony of death hit him full force,
The whale's demise consumed him like his own.
He fell at once in fever, overthrown,
Came to himself weeks later tucked in bed.
The whale, by then, for just as long, was dead,
The ship returned to port, the blubber boiled,
The whalebone cut and dried, her flesh despoiled.
Some lovely corsets were made up and sold.
The high society of Boston strolled
About the town, with ladies' flesh embraced
By that whale's baleen interlaced
With cotton binding. Then, that very week
They held a ball to celebrate their clique.
The theme was ladies white, and men in black,
And so the ladies came, dressed to attack,
Each wearing proudly her new whalebone gown
As white as baby teeth, as soft as down.
The mate, still suffering from his fevered fit,
Betook an action inappropriate,
And, shivering, showed up where he shouldn't be
Then scandalized their party with his plea:
"Dear ladies, take your dresses off!" he cried.
"The owner wants them back, the one who died."

A silence greeted him before the shock
Wore off, and then the laughter seemed to rock
The room before he was escorted to
The door. But just before they shoved him through,
A lady gasped, "My dress just got too tight!"
"Mine, too", another shrieked, and then a fight
Began between the ladies and their frocks.
They tried to rip them off, but fast as locks
They were shut in, the corsets tighter still!
Just then, a mystery wind blew through the hall,
Extinguishing the whale-oil lamps o'erall.
But darkness couldn't ease the horrid groan
Of all the ladies trapped in dresses sown
Of thread and satin and the right whale's jaw
That now compressed their organs like a claw.
To add to misery and woe, a rank
And fishlike odor, no, a reek, now stank
Throughout the room and made it hard to breathe.
Then came the part I still can't quite believe.
A huge, amorphous presence filled the hall,
A wet and hulking rage was sensed by all.
And then pealed forth a sound no human ear
Has heard before or since, a moan of fear,
A rumbling whine, a squeal that made the hair
Stand up, a shriek that floated in the air.
Then just as sudden all was still. One lamp,
It flickered on of its own will. The damp
And awful presence disappeared from view,
But every woman there had vanished, too.
The mate was then locked up, of course, for days.
But finally was released when in the bays
Of Boston missing womenfolk were found
All floating daintily and white, but drowned.
Still beautiful, each graceful as a swan,
Her dress fair, but the whalebone stays all gone.

LOUIS:
(After a moment)
How gross!

MARIE:
(The female eavesdropper)
(Comforting, with a slight German accent)
> But not a word of it is true.

DE COIGNY:
(The third eavesdropper)
It couldn't be.

ENGLISH SEAMAN: I'm with the lady, too.

RICHARD:
Why not?

LOUIS: Yes, why?

MARIE: Has word from Boston reached
Our ears of ladies washed up dead and beached?

FRENCH SEAMAN:
Of course, it would be covered up, a plague—

LOUIS:
Or else some other explanation vague.

MARIE:
(Preparing to leave)
Messieurs, so gullible!

FRENCH SEAMAN: I've seen a lot
At sea, and heard worse tales that I forgot.

RICHARD:
I never said that it was true, just that's
What I been told.

LOUIS: It must be true!

DE COIGNY:
(Trying to pull LOUIS away)

                                        These chats
Go on a little long for my taste—

LOUIS:
(Pulling free)

                                        No!

(To RICHARD*)*
Your story presupposes whales can grow
A soul in order to be ghosts.

RICHARD: I guess.

LOUIS:
I find that notion most intriguing.

MARIE: Yes,
But more disturbing.

LOUIS: In what way?

MARIE: We eat
A dozen animals a day. A feat
If they should come a-haunting us at night!

LOUIS:
Imagine that, Marie—

(Both MARIE *and* DE COIGNY *react to his use of her name in public.)*

LOUIS: —We had a bite
Of luncheon when our carriage stopped today.
My God! The souls in just one cassoulet!
Then escargot, a chicken, and some clams,
The beef, of course, the sausages and hams.
Why, we devour menageries!

FRENCH SEAMAN:
(Thinking of what he's eaten or would like to eat)
                                        There's veal,
And dove and salmon, porpoise, quail and eel—

LOUIS:
Wild bull, and boar, foie gras and blue-cooked pike,
And cormorant roast just the way I like—

FRENCH SEAMAN:
There's goat and goose and capon, bream and seal—

LOUIS:
And eggs! How many unborn souls we steal!
And not just eggs of fowls, but caviar!
A host of fishy souls in just one jar!
All kinds of seafood—skate and ray and shark.
More birds, like egret, heron, swan and lark.

RICHARD:
There's venison and turkey!

ENGLISH SEAMAN: Flounder!

RICHARD: Bear!

FRENCH SEAMAN:
There's tiger penis!

RICHARD: Possum!

FRENCH SEAMAN: Monkey!

ENGLISH SEAMAN: Hare!

LOUIS:
(Counting on his fingers)
Teal, partridge, crane, and guinea fowl,
Woodcock, warbler of Provence, and owl
Plus curlews, thrushes, buntings in a bunch
So many ghosts—and that was just for lunch!

MARIE:
Amusing, but it's all a wicked lie.

LOUIS:
Whoever found a phantom in a pie?

RICHARD:
It's not a lie—it is a tale. There's quite

A difference between the two, despite
What you may think.

LOUIS: The similarity
Is clear—they're both dishonest.

RICHARD: True, but we,
As God's flawed creatures crave a tale or two.
We don't need lies, but find a yarn will do.
The very Gospel texts themselves conflict
Each other's holy facts and contradict
In detail and chronology with stark
Changes in Christ's life from John to Mark.
And much of Matthew sounds like a rebuke
Of passages soon following in Luke.
But we believe them all—it is God's word,
And no dissenting voices will be heard.

LOUIS:
We do accept each verse as—Gospel truth!—
Embrace these stories from our very youth.
Perhaps we are too eager to discern
Divine authority—I often yearn—

DE COIGNY:
I'm loathe to interrupt theology—

MARIE:
Let's get a move on, dear, I have to pee.

LOUIS:
You're not a common seaman, sir.

RICHARD: I am
American, as common as a clam,
For each man there's of equal dignity.
No artificial aristocracy
Sets one apart, appoints the right to rule.

MARIE:
I'm tired, sweets, let's go.

DE COIGNY: This man's a fool.

LOUIS:
Are you implying here in France that things
Are misruled by divinely chosen kings?

RICHARD:
I've not been here a day, and yet I see
The people eating grass, in poverty.
While nobles like yourself—

LOUIS: Insult me, do!

RICHARD:
Gorge on exotic flesh, consume a zoo!

LOUIS:
Do you have any notion of my name?

FRENCH SEAMAN:
(Bowing down)
Take care! Shut up!

RICHARD: To me it's all the same.
We kicked King George across the sea
And have no earthly use for monarchy.

LOUIS:
The peasants here adore the King! Why just
Today, a turnip of a woman rushed
And threw herself headlong into the mire
At my feet. I asked her her desire,
Quite unperturbed. She said to me—a fire
Within her heart— "Just to embrace you, sire!"

RICHARD:
So what?

ENGLISH SEAMAN:
(Bowing down)
          You idiot!

LOUIS: You take a chance!

RICHARD:
I don't care if you are—

LOUIS:
(Overlapping)

                              I am—

LOUIS & RICHARD: —The King of France!

(Pause, as this sinks in for RICHARD. *He notices the*
SEAMEN *bowed low. He realizes he might be in trouble.)*

RICHARD:
The King—

LOUIS: Of France.

RICHARD: Louis Sixteen—

LOUIS: The same.
Perhaps—this known—you will respect my name—

RICHARD:
(Carefully)
I will afford it every courtesy—
If you will deign to do the same for me.

DE COIGNY:
See here! The King excuses ignorance,
But now you know his rank—

RICHARD: I'm not from France.

LOUIS:
Why, I could have your head!

MARIE: Dear, don't.

LOUIS:
I will!

RICHARD: Unless you are unjust, you won't.

(They all stare for a moment, apprehensive about LOUIS'
next move. He's apprehensive himself. The BARMAID *even*
runs away. Finally, LOUIS *breaks into a grin.)*

LOUIS:
I need to travel more! One always meets
The most unusual people in the streets!

I like this crass American, this rube
Who dares to treat me like I am a boob!
Your name, *Monsieur*—

RICHARD: Just call me Richard, please.

LOUIS:
No patronymic—

RICHARD: Cast it off. It frees
Me from my family name's imbroglio,
For lineage can be a trap, you know.

LOUIS:
Ah, none knows better, Richard, lad! Why are
You here in France? You've come so very far
To twit the royals.

RICHARD: You invited me.

LOUIS:
I did?

RICHARD: With every whaling family
That left Nantucket weeks ago to bring
Our skills at killing whales to France's king.

LOUIS:
Now that explains your cocky attitude!
You're here at my behest, how very rude
Of me! I asked you here to teach us how
To slaughter a cetacean like a cow.
Where are you docked?

RICHARD:
(Pointing)
                              Right over there.

LOUIS: May I
Request a little tour? I'd like to spy
On how you melt a giant down to oil.

RICHARD:
I'll happily instruct how whalers boil

The blubber, and explain the harpoon trade
(Holds out his hand)
To novices as long as I am paid.

LOUIS:
(After a tense moment, jovially)
You're so American! On Thursday then—

(RICHARD continues to hold out his hand.)

LOUIS:
Oh—in advance!

*(LOUIS gestures to DE COIGNY, who pays RICHARD.
RICHARD just stares at the money.)*

LOUIS: Some more.

(DE COIGNY pays RICHARD some more.)

RICHARD: See you at ten.
(Starts to leave, then stops.)
But wait—if he's the King, then you're—

DE COIGNY: The Queen.

RICHARD:
And no more lovely lady have I seen.

(MARIE is dumfounded.)

RICHARD:
Apologies if I o'er-reach my place
But in America a comely face
Is royalty enough for common men—

MARIE:
Apology accepted.
(After a moment, awkwardly waving him off)
                    Until then!

(RICHARD bows awkwardly and leaves with the money.)

LOUIS:
I am divinely chosen, don't you think—

MARIE:
(Pulling LOUIS *away from the* SEAMEN, *who quickly leave.)*
Of course, dear, but this country's on the brink
Of revolution and that kind of man
Is now born French, not just American.
I warned you France is changing, but this trip
You had to take. And so we watch them strip
The ornaments right off our carriage top
And trample them. What makes you think they'd stop
At that—

LOUIS: But you stayed calm and borrowed cloaks
From generous peasants—you're so quick!

MARIE: Nice folks.

LOUIS:
But did you have to shout that ugly rant
Against the Bourbon family—

MARIE: I can't
Apologize for what I did not mean
For I'm as much a woman as a queen.
You men force women into telling lies
Then chide us if our feelings we disguise.

LOUIS:
I know you saved our lives just now, my sweet.
They chased an empty carriage down the street.

MARIE:
The peasants love you still, but will you now
Believe me that the bourgeoisie won't bow—

LOUIS:
The peasants do eat grass—we need reform.
But I should get the credit for transform—
'Ing our society. If we can force
The nobles to agree to tax—divorce
Themselves from privileges—

DE COIGNY: Let's not forget,
I am still in the room.

LOUIS: I don't regret
Inviting you along, de Coigny, but
You're here to be my Equerry and not
To represent opinions of your class.

DE COIGNY:
You majesties—not just to save my ass—
I truly do concur with you about
That notion that we all must do without
Traditions of inequity if we
Are to survive as a society.
I am, however, rare among my breed,
For most aristocrats have not agreed.

MARIE:
Louis, don't taunt our friend the Duc—
The only noble doesn't make me puke.
For his advice will help convince the rest—

DE COIGNY:
The national assembly is a test—

LOUIS:
—That we would fail! I'll not assemble men
To vote against fair taxes once again!

DE COIGNY:
The composition of the group, the Third
Estate—

LOUIS:
(Giving DE COIGNY the finger)
          Up yours!
(Stomps out)

DE COIGNY: The King gave me the bird.

MARIE:
With you at least he's trying to be polite—
He farts to disagree with me at night.

We're too familiar, commonplace, for him.
He'd rather talk to oddities, a whim
Of late.

DE COIGNY: He once thought I was full of wit
But now he'll always do the opposite
Of what I say.

MARIE:
That whaler had his full
Attention, did you see? He pulled the wool
O'er Louis' eyes in nothing flat with just
Bad French, a smile, outrageous tales, robust
Delivery.

DE COIGNY: A handsome face...

MARIE:
(Grudgingly)

That, too.

DE COIGNY:
He's made as much impression upon you.

MARIE:
He is a man, and they're in short supply.
All men are boys before their Queen, and my
Own Louis' no exception to the rule.

DE COIGNY:
He is a man, down to the molecule.

MARIE:
All women want a man, that is their curse.
And men all want their kings, that's even worse.
And kings want gods to tell them what to do.

DE COIGNY:
I disagree! How sad if all that's true!

MARIE:
Each seeks someone with more authority
So they can shirk responsibility.

DE COIGNY:
This Richard's bold—as if he's on the stage.
Perhaps you could recruit him as your page
For amateur theatricals instead
Of making your poor, bashful husband tread
The boards.

MARIE: Poor Louis wasn't born to act,
But I'm on stage each moment—that's a fact.
The only time he plays a part is when he sneaks
About in quaint disguise and shyly peeks
Into his kingdom as a commoner.

DE COIGNY:
Just like tonight. It's tedious. But your
Performance as the queen is always deft.

(The SEAMEN *return and begin to change the set.)*

MARIE:
Of all my noble friends, thank God you're left!
The rest have since turned critic—bad reviews
Are all I get these days. Could not refuse
To go in public when I was with child,
And yet to show's indelicate, defiled.
My pregnancies were difficult ones, too,
But, of course, nobody ever knew.
I forge a fiction every second I'm alive.

DE COIGNY:
It's time to forge a new one as we strive
To get him to convene Estates General.

MARIE:
I had a clever thought that may appall
You quite a bit at first, but hear me out.
The First Estate, the nobles—too much clout.
The Second group, the clergy, go along
With what the nobles think.

DE COIGNY: The final throng,
The Third Estate, the bourgeoisie and ranks
Of peasants, love the King and give him thanks
For small reforms.

MARIE: They don't like me, I know,
But no one does. In any case, they show
The King support and want the nobles taxed.
And could win out if legal rules relaxed.

DE COIGNY:
I think I know where you will go with this.

MARIE:
If Louis can forget his prejudice,
Convene the Estates General with one
Small change—

DE COIGNY: What's that?

MARIE: I think it would be fun
To give the Third Estate a double count
Of delegates. They merit that amount
And then could overrule nobility
And church combined.

DE COIGNY: What silly sanctity
Has kept the three Estates just so for each—

MARIE:
Then you agree with me—you are a peach!

(DE COIGNY *helps* MARIE *out of her cloak, revealing her
regal finery.*)

DE COIGNY:
But how to get your husband to agree?

MARIE:
I'll think of something—leave that one to me.

(*The* SEAMAN *have changed the set to a rather nicely
appointed nun's cell in a Carmelite cloister. The* BARMAID
has become SISTER LOUISE, LOUIS' *elderly aunt, a nun.* DE

COIGNY *disappears.* LOUISE, *who is seated, and* MARIE,
who is not, stare at each other a moment, hostile.)

MARIE:
Bonjour, Madame.

LOUISE: Bonjour. A nice surprise.

MARIE:
We are in Normandy to analyze
The readiness of French warships. The fleet's
A favorite project of the King.

LOUISE: Mistreats
You, does he, bringing you along?

MARIE: No, we—

LOUISE:
My nephew played with boats when he was three.
He now has fleets of toys. But I'm concerned
For you, my dear. You've worked so hard and learned
To speak a French that's almost perfect, brought
An elegance to court I never thought
They knew in Austria. And though I'm cloi-
-Stered here, word has it that you don't enjoy
Versailles.

MARIE:
Oh, no, Madame. You have misheard.
Your nephew is the one who is referred
To as disturbed. *"L'etat, c'est moi"* was what
His great grandfather said—

LOUISE: I hope he's not
Considering a change of policy.
A king is still the state. The state is he.
He must not think of altering one whit!

MARIE:
Exactly what upsets him so! That's it!
You're so perceptive! He discerns a can-

-Cer here in France and feels it like a man
With tumors in his flesh.

LOUISE: Duc d'Orleans,
My nephew's handsome cousin—

MARIE: —Devil spawn—

LOUISE:
What's that?

MARIE: Don't let me interrupt.

LOUISE: The Duc,
Unlike Louis, is not the type to spook
So easily. A friendly warning, dear:
I've heard some say Duc d'Orleans would steer
This ship of state far better than your spouse.
Of course I don't agree at all—

MARIE: The louse!

LOUISE:
Pardon?

MARIE: Oh, nothing—just a little sneeze.

LOUISE:
It's most annoying.
(*Handing* MARIE *a handkerchief*)
                          Take a hankie, please.

MARIE:
My lord the King is not afraid, but sees
The kingdom fall to ruin and disease.
The country is in debt—now that I know—

LOUISE:
So glad you brought that up! May I bestow
Upon you some old maidenly advice?

MARIE:
I cherish what you say! Now, don't ask twice!

LOUISE:
The filtered tales that reach my cloistered ears
I'm sure are just the tip of what one hears
Out in the streets of Paris, at Versailles,
But as your aunt-in-law and elder, I
Believe my duty is to give to you
A brief precis of rumors that ensue.

MARIE:
I hang on tenterhooks, Madame. Proceed.

LOUISE:
I'll make an effort to condense the screed
That flies against you everywhere today.
Economy is not your strength, they say.
Your dressmaker, that Mademoiselle—

MARIE: Bertin.

LOUISE:
My correspondents just don't understand
How she can charge you twice the going rate!
And all those horses! My dear, you must hate
It said that "half her stable she should sell
Since, truth be told, she doesn't ride that well".
Extravaganzas at Versailles, your fetes—
You don't mind, do you?

MARIE: Madame, no regrets!

LOUISE:
Your parties are much better known for waste
Than wit, imagination, grace or taste.
Again, these aren't my words—I don't attend—

MARIE:
You're not invited.

LOUISE: No, for I must spend
My life—

MARIE: —Eternity—

LOUISE: —In cloistered bliss.
Just think of all the gossip that I miss!
I tell you this for your own benefit—
That people call you "Madame Deficit".

MARIE:
Madame Louise, I'm glad I can rely
On older people pleased to verify
That libels such as these abound in France.
I'm grateful that you shared your confidence
And hope that you won't mind if I share too.

LOUISE:
Of course not!

MARIE: Good. Here's what I've heard of you.
From Paris our Lieutenant of Police
Reports to me each morning every piece
Of slander that is circulating there
About such serious matters as my hair.
As sad and crazy as it sounds, some prigs
Discuss all day the scandal of my wigs!
While I'm amused that people find my clothes
A more important topic than expos-
-Ing how the clergy live in luxury—
Despite supposed vows of poverty—
One sordid bit of calumny does grate
Upon my royal nerves. It seems that late-
-Ly Antoinette the Queen hates motherhood
So very much she's joined the brotherhood
Of pederasts in practice, goes down south,
And satisfies her husband in her mouth.
This traitor to our race now takes no chance
And swallows all the future kings of France!
I must return this gossip's gunnery,
Which we've traced back right to this nunnery.

LOUISE:
(After a moment, caught, furious)

We cannot have a queen who's like a punk
And relishes the sour taste of spunk.

MARIE:
That's earthy language for a nun! But no
Surprise—hypocrisy will always show.
Oh, have I touched a tender nerve? Don't squirm—
We know I know you know the taste of sperm.
But is it sour all the time or does
It change with what men eat— My Louis' was
Quite sweet. I'm sure you've sampled creamy, tangy,
    tart,
And spicy, salty—served you a la carte.
Or are exotic flavors more your style?
Like wormwood, gall, or garlic—no fear, I'll
Go on and on and on—I won't be dumb
Before a gourmand in cuisine of cum.

LOUISE:
It's been described to me by wayward nuns
Who've scuttled off and been returned. It stuns
Me that you'd speak to me in such a tone,
When all I've done is offer help. You've shown
As little gratitude as naughty girls
Who show up here so I can salve the world's
Abuse of their soft innocence with cures
I've learned. Then—back they run into the sewers!
I've never tasted men nor touched their skin.
Just smelled on girls the bitter whiff of sin.

MARIE:
You dare complain of tone and courtesy?
I've stood, you've sat—

LOUISE: Well, I have pleurisy.

MARIE:
And you have yet to offer me a chair.
Who's queen here, Sister?

LOUISE:
(Starting to get up)

                    I need air!

MARIE:
(Forcing LOUISE *back down into the chair)*
Oh, no you don't! Stay seated for your health.
I won't forget you've offered me a wealth
Of information here today. I owe
You an intelligence, ergo:
My Louis sends affectionate regards
And, if you weren't a cloistered nun, milliards
Of kisses. But he also hopes that you
Will not get too distraught or misconstrue
His thought when you hear that he plans to call
A gathering of the Estates General.

LOUISE:
But that would be the end!

MARIE: Of what, Madame?

LOUISE:
The monarchy! Why, must I diagram
This country's problem for you, silly child—
Convene all three Estates? France would go wild!

MARIE:
He said to say that he'd find beautiful
A monarchy that's constitutional.

LOUISE:
(Gasping)
He mustn't! I shall tell him—please convey—

MARIE:
Impart your wisdom in your usual way,
With whispered rumors, falsehoods and canards
That find their way from Carmelite dooryards
Across the country then at last to court.

LOUISE:
I cannot breathe—please call—!

MARIE:
(Doing nothing to help)

                                        I shall report
To Louis that Madame is feeling spry—
I pray that will not be another lie.

(Lights fade on LOUISE *gasping and struggling in her chair. The* SEAMEN *appear and begin to change the set.* DE COIGNY *appears and goes to* MARIE, *helping her into an elegant traveling cloak.)*

DE COIGNY:
She took the bait?

MARIE: The hook is in her gut.
Despite my taunts, she won't keep her mouth shut.

(The SEAMEN *carry the struggling* LOUISE *away in her chair, then return to transforming the set.* DE COIGNY *hands* MARIE *a gardenia that she affixes to her hair.)*

DE COIGNY:
But will the King react as you predict?

MARIE:
Within mere days, he'll have his conscience pricked.
When all of France believes he's on the verge
Of calling the assembly, he'll emerge
To meet their expectations and proclaim
A policy to set their hearts aflame.

(The SEAMEN *continue transforming the set until it is the deck of an American whaling vessel. Sound effects, seagulls, etc., complete the mis-en-scene.* LOUIS, *now wearing his royal traveling regalia, appears with* RICHARD, *who is giving him a tour of the ship.)*

RICHARD:
Then after I harpoon the mighty beast
He tows the boat an hour or two at least.

It's usually on the surface, but they sound
Sometimes—that's dive, to you—and can't be found
Till they come up to breathe.

LOUIS: A whale breathes air?

DE COIGNY:
But isn't it a fish?

RICHARD: That's true, but they're
In many ways much more akin to us.
I've never known a fish made noise or fuss,
But once I heard a whale scream.

LOUIS: My God!

RICHARD:
I had bad luck, fell from a boat. I trod
The water for a bit, then saw the whale,
Harpooned, exhausted, aimed at me—full sail!
I sank beneath the waves then heard a boom
That shivered through the water like the doom
Of all the world. Some clicks and then a wheeze.
The creature died as nicely as you please.

LOUIS:
Marie, did you hear that' The whale screamed.

MARIE:
You're sure it wasn't something that you dreamed?

RICHARD:
Oh, when I dream, I hope it's not of fish.

MARIE:
Well, then, Monsieur, I hope you get your wish.

RICHARD:
(Nervous, pointing)
The tryworks here, are where we boil the skin,
The blubber full of oil, and put it in
Those barrels over there.

LOUIS: But you don't cook
The spermaceti oil?

RICHARD: You've read a book
Or two on whaling!

LOUIS: Studied up a bit.
My knowledge shouldn't be inadequate
If I'm to found this industry in France.
But tell me please, so I that can advance.
In French it's cachalot, in English "sperm".
Can you explain the meaning of this term?

RICHARD:
(Somewhat embarrassed in front of MARIE*)*
It's technical biology—

MARIE: Of course.

RICHARD:
Within the creature's skull he stores the source
Of reproductive function—

LOUIS: Please speak plain.

RICHARD:
His head is full of seed! And when you drain
It out, you see it takes up all the room!

MARIE:
He's just like any man, then, I assume.

LOUIS:
Proportionally, Marie—

DE COIGNY: Imagine that!

MARIE:
Then Louis, you could never wear a hat!

LOUIS:
The spermaceti oil is why this trade
Is worth so much to us. So far it's made
Rich men of Quaker paupers overseas.

DE COIGNY:
How is this trade so lucrative?

RICHARD: We squeeze
The money out of every whale. The oil
Of spermaceti, if it doesn't spoil,
Becomes the finest candle wax on earth.
(Gives them white tapers.)
It doesn't smoke or stink, and so it's worth
The weight of many tapers made by bees.
No tallow holds a candle next to these.
I sometimes wonder whether it would vex
A whale to know we get light from his sex.
But sperm whales offer more to us than wax.
(Finds some oil and puts a few drops on their hands)
The whale oil from the blubber also acts
As lubricant that's slick and thick as slime
But doesn't get all clotted over time.

MARIE:
It's nice and slippery.

LOUIS:
(Grabbing MARIE's greasy hand in his own.)
                              And makes me feel
As if my hand had turned into an eel.

(MARIE gives a little shriek of pleasure.)

DE COIGNY:
(Trying to figure out where to clean his hand)
But as an oil, it's hard to get off, right?

LOUIS:
If you haven't used it yet for that, you might.

(LOUIS giggles naughtily with MARIE.)

RICHARD:
(Wiping his hands on his dirty shirt)
Oh, I just wipe it on my shirt.

DE COIGNY: We can't.

RICHARD:
Well, sure you can.
(Grabs DE COIGNY*'s hands and wipes them on his own*
*[*RICHARD*'s] shirt.)*

MARIE: Oh, my!

DE COIGNY: Oh, dear!

RICHARD: Just plant
`Em here.

*(*DE COIGNY, LOUIS, *and* MARIE *all wipe their hands all*
over RICHARD*'s shirt.)*

RICHARD: I might catch fire—I'm volatile!

DE COIGNY:
What do you mean?

LOUIS: That whale oil's flammable!
Do you have lamps?

*(*RICHARD *produces a lit lamp.)*

LOUIS:
You see how clean it burns—
Compare it to the olive Europe spurns
In favor of this liquid gold. This light
Will lead us out of economic night
Into a bright and prosperous new day.

MARIE:
I feel a bit left out.

LOUIS: What's that you say?

MARIE:
This fish does not make whalebone, does it?

RICHARD: No.

MARIE:
Then pardon me if I'm not all aglow.

RICHARD:
(Inspecting her buttons, perhaps too closely)

These ivory buttons are all sperm whale teeth.
You scratch a woman's clothes, a whale's beneath.

MARIE:
I beg your pardon! Am I zaftig, then?

LOUIS:
No German, please!

RICHARD: I'm sorry, don't—

MARIE: You men!
It's all economy with you!

LOUIS: Why not?
This fish is gold!

MARIE: I won't move from this spot
Till you acknowledge that each candle fire,
Each lamp, is some poor whale's funeral pyre.
(Starts popping off her buttons.)
And now I realize with every breath
That I've bedecked myself with pretty death!

LOUIS:
Marie, a whale's a soul-less animal!

MARIE:
Is their blood warm or cold?

RICHARD: It's hot.

MARIE: You call
That soul-less?

LOUIS: Yes, just like a cow or horse.
And you eat them quite happily.

MARIE: Of course.
I know I'm oversensitive, it's just—

LOUIS:
I want to go a-whaling.

MARIE: No!

LOUIS: I must!
You can't control my every move, you know.

MARIE:
What's that supposed to mean?

LOUIS: I'll show
You later what my auntie wrote to me
About your visit to her nunnery.
You'll not shame me to make me do your will.

MARIE:
Oh, Louis, for the love of France—

LOUIS: Be still!
Please don't forget that I'm the king, not you.
And I'm the one who's really French, now, too.

(When MARIE *sulks:)*

LOUIS:
Oh, sweetheart, you're so pretty when you sulk.
I know you mean well with your plots, the bulk
Of which aren't too hare-brained. But I'm the one
Who's got the plan for France. And whaling's done
America some good. Just think of all
The products come from whales—

RICHARD: We left one small
But precious product out.

LOUIS: What's that?

RICHARD: It's this.
(Plucking the gardenia from MARIE*'s hair)*
A flower's scent can live in ambergris
For years and years, when otherwise it dies
In days.

LOUIS: Of course! The fish delights the eyes
But even more the nose, we may presume.
A sperm whale fixes fragrance in perfume

With ambergris, a substance pure as frank-
—Incense. But where's it come from, Monsieur Yank?

RICHARD:
Nobody knows. Sometimes it's found afloat
Upon the sea. I heard an anecdote
About a whale who puked it up when caught—

LOUIS:
My God! To think this substance highly sought
Is from the indigestion of a whale!
Miraculous these creatures are! Let's sail!

RICHARD:
(Looking at the sky)
A gale is on the way. Let's wait.

LOUIS: How soon
May I accompany your ship?

RICHARD: At noon
Tomorrow we'll take to the open sea.
Of course, there is the matter of the fee.

LOUIS:
(Laughs, hands RICHARD *money)*
You hear, Marie' I'm off! So buy a dress,
A chateau in Provence—it's taken less
To make you feel better in the past.
Think of all the jewels you've amassed.
Forget Estates General. Leave that to men.
Instead, go mount a little play again.

*(*LOUIS *taking* RICHARD*'s arm as they leave together.)*

LOUIS:
I take it as a sign from God that we
Have met. We'll change the country's destiny!

DE COIGNY:
(After LOUIS *and* RICHARD *have left.)*
So much for that.

MARIE: Oh, shut up.

DE COIGNY: Now we're sunk.

MARIE:
What kind of attitude is that? My trunk
Of tricks is far from bare. We fail?
Oh, no, there's many ways to skin a whale.
As tired as I am of running things
And sick to death of playing queens and kings,
I'm still the mistress of my master's mood.
Remember that poor peasant who was rude
Enough to beg him for a king's embrace?

DE COIGNY:
The frumpy dumpling with the pock-marked face?

MARIE:
A country maid who truly loves her king—
Her love of gold's a much more useful thing.
A coin I sent ahead to work its spell
Bought my poor Louis happiness as well.

DE COIGNY:
I see you haven't really lost your touch.

MARIE:
Manipulating Louis? Don't take much.

DE COIGNY:
I often think you'd make a stronger king.
It's what France needs as much as anything.

MARIE:
It is my lot to work behind the scenes—
We must resort to supernatural means.

DE COIGNY:
Religious hoaxes once again?

MARIE: Why not?

DE COIGNY:
To have him heal fake scrofula has got
To be the cheapest trick we've ever played.

MARIE:
It worked.

DE COIGNY: We can't repeat ourselves.

MARIE: This trade
In blubber seems so mystical to him.
I wonder if we can't transform his whim
Into some sort of message from beyond.
Those seamen's ghostly tales of which he's fond
Might be the means we're seeking.

DE COIGNY: And that man!

MARIE:
Profoundly influential! If you can
Would you approach him on the Queen's behalf?

DE COIGNY:
And ask him to do what? He'll only laugh
In raucous disbelief at our intrigues.

MARIE:
I have a feeling he might travel leagues
To please the Queen.

DE COIGNY: Or earn a little cash.

MARIE:
More to the point, of course.

DE COIGNY: Would he be rash
Enough to back up our outrageous lies?

MARIE:
Let's call them tales, they're lies, but in disguise.
I think he likes to fib. Just be discreet,
And flatter him, arrange for us to meet.
As Louis said, I'll have a play put on.

The whaler as Tartuffe, the King—Orgon.
It's perfect casting, no?

LOUIS:
(*Appearing with* RICHARD)
                                        Marie, my sprite!
I want to get a healthy rest tonight!

MARIE:
I'll sing you chanties till we fall asleep.

LOUIS:
Tomorrow we'll be sailing on the deep.
(*To* MARIE.)
He just confessed that he's the bastard son
Of that red-headed—

RICHARD: —Thomas Jefferson.

MARIE:
(*Giving* DE COIGNY *a significant look*)
Monsieur, you're clearly all that we could wish
For in a guide to take us chasing fish.

LOUIS:
(*As they leave*)
When we get home, I'll spank your little butt.

MARIE:
(*Flirtatiously*)
I know that I deserve it, dear.

LOUIS:
(*Affectionately*)
                                        You slut!

(LOUIS *and* MARIE *disappear.* DE COIGNY *regards*
RICHARD *for a moment.*)

DE COIGNY:
Now—Thomas Jefferson?

RICHARD: Yes, you heard right.
He's quite an active gentleman at night.

DE COIGNY:
The author of democracy, they say.

RICHARD:
At home he's well regarded in that way.

DE COIGNY:
It does explain a lot.

RICHARD:
                                    Regarding me?

DE COIGNY:
You're not the bumpkin you pretend to be.

RICHARD:
A natural son pretends his whole life
Because his mum is not his father's wife.

DE COIGNY:
Your French has much improved in recent days
You're educated, too.

RICHARD:
(Shrugs)
                              My father pays.
But I have been a whaler for two years,
Not just to feed my loving father's fears.
Since I was born, I've felt the sea was home.
Out on the water, cutting through the foam,
You cannot hide from God. It's true. It's pure.

DE COIGNY:
Have you spent time in seminary?

RICHARD: You're
Good! Yale Divinity, in fact.

DE COIGNY: It shows.

RICHARD:
Dropped out, of course.

DE COIGNY: And that shows, too.

RICHARD: I chose
A more adventurous path to meet my God.

DE COIGNY:
You'd like to meet a Queen?

RICHARD: Alone?

DE COIGNY: No prod-
-Ding needed here! Yes, late tonight. I'll send
A message telling where.

RICHARD: You can depend
On me to serve the Queen.

DE COIGNY: It isn't what
You think. So please try not to get all hot.
She hopes that you will do a homily
About the precepts of democracy.

RICHARD:
For whom?

DE COIGNY: The King.

RICHARD: How much?

DE COIGNY: Negotiable.
Our King is very bright but gullible.
The price goes up if you'll embellish truth.

RICHARD:
No problem there.

DE COIGNY: Quite so. I blame your youth.

(Departing, as the lights change)

DE COIGNY:
I hope I may be frank: you lie with ease.

RICHARD:
(Alone)
But lies give birth to greater verities.

*(Lighting on RICHARD changes. It is the next day, still on
the ship, but now sound effects and lighting make it clear the*

ship is under sail. LOUIS *arrives with* MARIE, *both wearing*
their version of "whaling attire".)

LOUIS:
The dream awoke me hours before the dawn,
And then I couldn't sleep again, just yawn
And shiver at the awful memory.

MARIE:
A nightmare? Can you give a summary?
I'd give a treasury of louis d'ors
To find a remedy to end your snores.

LOUIS:
I stood upon a treeless plain alone.
No rock or refuge from relentless sun,
And yet a thunder grumbled through the sky.
The sound grew louder, shook the earth, and I
Prepared to run but didn't know which way
The roar was coming from. The grand melee
Surrounded me and clouds of dust arose,
Encircling like a noose can interpose
Betwixt a man and life. And then I saw
The source of the commotion—stared in awe
And panic at the sight! A herd of sheep—

MARIE:
But counting mutton usually helps you sleep!

LOUIS:
It wasn't only ewes and rams and lambs—
A herd of veal followed with their dams!
And then a thousand sucklings, boars and sows
Enlisted in this force of sheep and cows!
And while the vanguard thundered on the ground,
Above me in the air I heard a sound—
A million flapping wings and angry squawks
Of chickens, pigeons, guineas, geese and hawks!
A cloud of vicious birds a mile high
With every razor beak aimed at my eye!

I tried to duck the ducks, and got my wish
Until the air around me filled with fish!
The salmon, trout, shark, jellyfish and pike,
The porpoise, tuna, sturgeon, and the like
All swam as if the very atmosphere
Had turned to water, then one bit my ear!
The first blood drawn, the signal to attack,
They tore off tidbits of my legs, my back,
My scalp, my hands outstretched to ward them off—
No use—they rushed me like a feeding trough!
All denizens air and sea, yes, every beast
A famished epicure and I the feast.
Although my eyes were gobbled first, I still
Could see the hungry creatures have their fill.
They butchered me with beak and tooth and claw,
My flesh all gone, my bones were left to gnaw.
Though somehow conscious, I knew I was dead
And not a bit remained except my head
A-staring at the sky with empty eyes,
The sockets meanwhile nibbled by some flies.

MARIE:
No wonder you could not get back to bed—
A pillow's not much good for just a head!

LOUIS:
What could it mean, a dream this dark and fell?

MARIE:
Perhaps that yesterday you ate too well.

LOUIS:
You could be right, I should have eaten less.
I am experiencing queasiness.

MARIE:
Now that you mention it, I've never seen
Your royal person look so very—

(LOUIS, *suddenly quite seasick, stumbles to the side and
vomits.*)

MARIE:
(Signaling to DE COIGNY, *who appears.)*
                                        —Green.

Oh, Louis, dear!
(Comforting him)

RICHARD: He'll get his sea-legs soon.

DE COIGNY:
Not soon enough! It's now late afternoon
And we've been underway for several hours.

RICHARD:
Whales don't swim close to shore to smell the flowers.

(Sound effect of a whale spouting. MARIE, *tending to* LOUIS
at the rail, notices, but DE COIGNY *and* RICHARD *do not.)*

MARIE:
Excuse me, but—

DE COIGNY: This jaunt is for the King
He's been so sick he'll miss the whole thing.
(To LOUIS)
Your Majesty, should we turn back?

LOUIS:
(Weakly, then returning to puking)
                                        Oh, no!

RICHARD:
You see, a most determined King—bravo!

DE COIGNY:
Harpoon a porpoise—small, but that will be
Enough to satisfy the royalty.

MARIE:
I thought that spout of water meant—

RICHARD: I can't
Produce a whale out of a hat. They're scant
This close to Europe nowadays. We're plucked

These northern waters clean, so now we're fucked
Unless we go to southern seas.

DE COIGNY: Then why
Mislead the King, build up his hopes and try
To find a whale where there are none?

MARIE:
(Looking out)

                                                There goes—!

RICHARD:
They migrate here sometimes.

MARIE: Oh, there she—

*(A splash of water from a spouting whale comes over the side
and soaks RICHARD.)*

MARIE: —Blows!

*(MARIE signals DE COIGNY, who attends LOUIS as MARIE
goes to RICHARD.)*

RICHARD:
The whale has baptized me—
(Revels in the wet)

                           —And cleansed my sin,
Prepared me for the ritual I begin.

AMERICAN WHALER:
(Rushing by, disappearing)
There she blows! Harpooner, to the boat!

RICHARD:
I know we said last night that—

MARIE: I outvote
You on this one.
(Gives him money)

                    Here's more incentive, dear.
Go out and catch a nasty whale—no fear!

ANOTHER WHALER:
(Rushing by, disappearing.)
There she blows! A big one, too!

MARIE: Be off!

RICHARD:
It's not just for the cash—!

MARIE: Don't make me scoff!

RICHARD:
A whaler takes his life into his hand
Each and every time the boats are manned.
We lost the mate to sharks the last time out—
I hope that I return—

MARIE:
(Pointing)
                              Another spout!

(One last look at MARIE, then RICHARD dashes off.)

MARIE:
What is a man, next to a nation's pain?
The truth? I'll never see his sort again.

DE COIGNY:
(Calling MARIE.)
Your Majesty!

MARIE:
(Going to LOUIS.)
                    Louis! The boats are down!
They're in pursuit! Lift up your royal crown!

LOUIS:
(Trying to look, very wobbly.)
They are— Oh, no!
(Just lifting his head makes him vomit again. He drops his head.)

MARIE:
That's all right, dear. Just rest.
We'll tell you what we see. Don't be distressed.

DE COIGNY:
The fish is on the surface, unawares.

MARIE:
The boats are pulling closer—

DE COIGNY: Say your prayers—

MARIE:
The boat that Richard's in is first in line.
Harpoon is raised—

DE COIGNY: He throws it hard! It's—!

MARIE: Fine!
He's hit it on the back!

DE COIGNY: I think it stuck!

MARIE:
The whale reacts by plunging!

DE COIGNY: Now, good luck!
The line attached is whipping out—!

MARIE: There's smoke!

DE COIGNY:
It didn't dive below!

MARIE: But goes for broke
Upon the surface of the sea, and tows
The boat like we would pull a toy. The throes
Of battle are begun! Oh, my!

DE COIGNY: What's that? It's vast!

MARIE:
The tail, I think! It's taller than a mast!

DE COIGNY:
Now, don't exaggerate!

MARIE: I'm not—it's big!

DE COIGNY:
It's gone. It got away.

MARIE: That whirligig
Is spinning still—the line remains stuck fast.
The whale dove beneath the waves and cast
Itself into the deep.

DE COIGNY:
                        So now we wait—
The whale is in the boat like so much bait.

MARIE:
The line is playing out—but, no, it's slack.
You think it broke—

(Sound of the whalers in the boat shouting)

DE COIGNY:
(Peering)
                     What's wrong?

MARIE: The whale turned back!
It's coming up! The men peer in the wave
Beneath the boat with fear, but what can save
Them from the awful monster down below?

DE COIGNY:
I see a shape! It's black and huge!

MARIE: They run—!

DE COIGNY:
But where— There's nowhere they can go!

MARIE: They're done-
-For!
(Screams, then stares in horror)

DE COIGNY: It burst up directly underneath
The boat! The fragile craft within the teeth
Of the Leviathan! The men fly all
Like puppets to the sky—

MARIE: Oh, Dick—!

DE COIGNY: Then fall!

(Sound of a splash in a separate area of the stage, RICHARD *falls into view on a wire or bungee cord. His clothes are wet, and he "swims" in the air, struggling to the surface of the water.)*

LOUIS:
(Moaning)
Where's Richard now?

*(*RICHARD *"swims" to the surface of the water [a slightly higher level in the air].)*

DE COIGNY: I see him!

MARIE: There he is!

RICHARD:
Now, look sharp lads! He's coming back! It's his
Chance for revenge!

DE COIGNY: The other boats row close
To save the drowning boys.

RICHARD: He's bellicose,
This bastard!

MARIE: It's among the floating men.
What mischief will it make?

DE COIGNY: The tail!

(For a fraction of a moment, a shadow passes between RICHARD *and the light that illuminates him.* RICHARD *closes his eye for a prayer.)*

RICHARD:
(Opening his eyes, after the shadow passes)
                              Amen!

(Sounds of a man's scream, then a giant smack of the tail upon the water. RICHARD *reacts to the sight.)*

MARIE:
Oh, that poor man!

DE COIGNY: It crushed him with its tail!

(RICHARD *"swims" and finds his harpoon.*)

MARIE:
It's circling back!

RICHARD: Come on, you beast! Vile whale!

DE COIGNY:
Now what's he doing? Taunting it?

RICHARD: Get me!

MARIE:
Distracting it to let the others be!

RICHARD:
You ton of blubber, fiend the devil sent,
I challenge you—I'm in your element!
Now fight a man who knows you well. Come glide
This way so I can stick this in your hide!

DE COIGNY:
Out of his mind!

MARIE: It's headed straight his way!

DE COIGNY:
The mouth—!

MARIE: It's opening!

DE COIGNY: That vast array
Of monstrous teeth!

MARIE: The mighty jaws agape!

DE COIGNY:
It's closing in!

MARIE: But can he still escape?

RICHARD:
Now that's it, brute! You dare destroy our boat—
I'll pay you back and shove this down your throat!

MARIE:
No, Richard, please!

DE COIGNY: Swim sideways, fool!

RICHARD: Come on!

DE COIGNY:
Get out of there!

MARIE: That mouth!

RICHARD:
(Lunging with his harpoon)
                                   Die, beast!

MARIE:
(A scream)
                                        He's gone!

(The light on RICHARD instantly goes out and he disappears from view. DE COIGNY and MARIE and peer silently for a moment.)

MARIE:
He's—

DE COIGNY: —Definitely—

MARIE: —Gone.

DE COIGNY: It swallowed him.

MARIE:
It couldn't have.

DE COIGNY: But otherwise he'd swim
Or float away. Dead or alive, we'd see.
He wouldn't sink.

MARIE: Then he's alive.

DE COIGNY: Can't be.

MARIE:
Like Jonah, he's alive inside the whale!

DE COIGNY:
The crushing teeth—!

MARIE: Be quiet! Most men are frail
And don't survive such shocks. But Richard's strong—

DE COIGNY:
Now, even so, he won't last very long.
He's sentenced to a horrid death as food
To that great beast. Confined in solitude—

MARIE:
Then we must get him out!
(Peering)
                                      A new harpoon
Is sticking in its side!

DE COIGNY: That's opportune—
The fish is rolling on its back!

MARIE: It's dead—
Or dying, isn't it?

LOUIS:
(Lifting his head)
                        It's overfed—
A mighty stomach ache.

MARIE: No, dear, that's you.

DE COIGNY:
They're stabbing it with lances.

MARIE: Then it's true—

LOUIS:
He can be saved!

DE COIGNY: Your majesties, I must
Diminish hope. He's surely dead, just trust
Me on this one.

(As DE COIGNY *talks about* RICHARD's *plight,* RICHARD
*appears in light, still suspended about four feet above the
stage. He struggles as if he is confined, he strains to breathe.
Low level bangs, booms, and clicks can be heard: the internal
sounds of the whale dying.)*

DE COIGNY: For even if the jaws
Don't masticate, defy the natural laws
That govern nourishment, the belly's not
A cozy habitat that's ever sought
By any prey. There will be little air,
The lack of which will certainly impair
His chances of survival in that hell.

(The ACIDS *[two men] appear standing below the suspended*
RICHARD, *and begin their work.)*

DE COIGNY:
But should he find some air and breathe it well,
He's only prolonged agony and pain.
The stomach is an acid hurricane
That buffets all within till it's consumed.
When that begins, poor Richard's surely doomed.
His clothing can't protect him very much,
And soon will be in tatters.

(The ACIDS *rip away most of* RICHARD's *clothing, leaving
pale, ragged remnants.)*

DE COIGNY: Bile and such
Will then attack his skin. He'll bleach at first,
In slow and torturous pain, dissolve at worst.
They'll eat at him until there's not a shred
Of dermis left, and yet he's still not dead.

(The ACIDS *stroke* RICHARD's *skin, leaving white marks,
until all his skin is bright, dead white.)*

DE COIGNY:
Then simultaneously, his hair will melt
Until there's not a whisker on his pelt.

A closer shave than barbers can perform,
The smoothest of his life, perhaps too warm.

(The ACIDS *pull off* RICHARD's *hair, beard and eyebrows,
leaving pale baldness.)*

DE COIGNY:
He'll close his eyes as tightly as he can,
But these corrosives infiltrate a man
Through every crevice, every tiny pore.
So soon he will be blinded evermore.

(The ACIDS *stroke* RICHARD's *closed eyes, leaving them
open and staring.)*

DE COIGNY:
But evermore won't be so very long,
For even if our Richard is as strong
As iron, bold as brass or hard as steel—

(The ACIDS *spin* RICHARD *on the rope. He goes into a fetal
position.)*

DE COIGNY:
Eventually he'll soften as a meal,
Becoming one with his enormous host
And we will only know him as a ghost.

(The lights go out on RICHARD *and the* ACIDS.*)*

LOUIS:
(Staggering but rallying)
Then we will save him if it's possible
From dying in this way most horrible!
(Calling to the whalers in the boats.)
I want that whale's stomach brought to me!

DE COIGNY:
You haven't heard a word, your Majesty!
He's whale-chow now, he couldn't be alive!

LOUIS:
We must have faith that somehow he'll survive.

Last night I got a warning this would be:
My gruesome nightmare was a prophecy.

MARIE:
But if your dream comes true, we'll find his head
And nothing more. It's sad, but so—he's dead.
Not even kings can rule over death.
Our Richard's surely drawn his final breath.

(The two WHALERS *rather reluctantly bring the whale's stomach to* LOUIS. *It is disgusting: huge and slimy, covered with blood.)*

LOUIS:
Look, there it is! The whale's enormous gut!
Just put it on the deck so you can cut
It open.

DE COIGNY: This is futile!

MARIE: And it's gross!
There's blood! It stinks! Louis, don't stand so close!

LOUIS:
We can't be squeamish and still save his life!

(Movement from inside the stomach)

LOUIS:
It moved! He's still alive! Who has a knife?

WHALER:
I've got one, but—

DE COIGNY: That's just a reflex nerve.

LOUIS:
(Grabbing the knife)
Then he who would be King must also serve!

*(*LOUIS *hacks open the stomach. Fluids pour out.)*

MARIE:
Oh, Louis, no! The blood! That outfit's new!

LOUIS:
Now, Richard, friend, as foul fluids spew
Recall the words of he who fished for men:
To follow me you must be born again!

(The moment that LOUIS cuts a big enough slit in the stomach, RICHARD sits bolt upright through the hole, gulping air. LOUIS jumps back and gasps, as do the others, for RICHARD looks awful. Not only is he covered with blood and fluids like a newborn, his skin is stark white and there's not a hair on his body. A second later, he reaches out his hands to feel his way—because he is now blind. The shock of this violent movement, combined with the powerful reek of the stomach's interior, is too much for the already queasy LOUIS. He dashes to the rail and vomits again.)

MARIE:
Oh, Richard!

DE COIGNY: God, he lives!

(RICHARD reacts to MARIE's voice, reaching blindly for her.)

MARIE: But he's so weak!
Let's wipe him clean! Get rags! Dear, can you speak?

(RICHARD turns toward MARIE and tries to talk, but all that comes out of his mouth is a strange booming, banging sound—the sound of the dying whale. Everyone stares at RICHARD, then at each other. Even LOUIS turns back from retching at the rail. RICHARD makes whale-like clicking noises, then another mournful boom that echoes as the lights fade to black.)

END OF ACT ONE

ACT TWO

(Versailles. DE COIGNY, LOUIS *and* MARIE)

DE COIGNY:
How fares your houseguest?

LOUIS: Well, he didn't die,
But won't eat, so we brought him to Versailles.

MARIE:
Louis devotes himself to Richard. None
May come between him and his long-lost son.

LOUIS:
No delicacy that our chefs have made
Has tempted him one bit. He's like a shade
Of his old self. He's blind and losing weight,
And not a single hair grows on his pate.

MARIE:
He hasn't said a word, just makes those sounds,
Those haunting moans and booms. His case confounds
Our doctors—treatments come to no avail.

DE COIGNY:
He's their first patient swallowed by a whale!
The second man in history to live
Through that. So judging from the first, forgive
Me, please, but you can bet your miniver
He'll soon be preaching doom to Nineveh!

LOUIS:
It is a miracle that he's not dead,
But what is going on inside his head?

(DE COIGNY and MARIE exchange a knowing look.)

MARIE:
It's hard to tell, with all those clicks and hums.
I'm sure he'll speak again.

(The moaning/booming sound is heard.)

LOUIS: Hush, here he comes.

*(Still uttering his moan/boom, RICHARD is escorted by a
SERVANT. RICHARD has been dressed for court, in finery
unlike anything he's ever known. He is still bald and
bleached, and holds onto the SERVANT with one hand and
gropes blindly before him with the other.)*

LOUIS:
Good morning, Richard, son. Had breakfast yet?

SERVANT
No, Your Majesty, he hasn't et.

LOUIS:
(Taking RICHARD's hands, loudly)
You poor boy, do you still insult our chef?

MARIE:
My dear, I think he's blind and dumb, not deaf.

(LOUIS embraces RICHARD.)

DE COIGNY:
(Quietly, to MARIE)
That pallor's rather fetching, don't you think?

LOUIS:
(Not so loud)
Let's ask the chef to make something to drink.
And then some seafood: octopus and shrimp.

DE COIGNY:
So bald and smooth—!

LOUIS: And scallops—mustn't scrimp!

RICHARD:
(Transitioning from his whale sounds)
Sssss! Ssss!

MARIE:
(Quietly, to DE COIGNY.*)*
You are depraved. Please don't incite me so!

LOUIS:
He's trying to talk!

DE COIGNY:
(Quietly)
                    I'm getting vertigo!

LOUIS:
He said a word. At least I think he did.
If you'd shut up!

DE COIGNY: Oh, sorry.

LOUIS: He said—

RICHARD: Sssssquid.

LOUIS:
Now what was that? Speak up. That wasn't clear.

DE COIGNY:
To me it sounds like "squid"—

MARIE: How very queer.

LOUIS:
Oh, not at all! Do you want squid, my lad?

RICHARD:
Squid. Hungry.

LOUIS: Yes, of course. We're very glad
You're talking now. So—anything you want!
A squid, a school of fish, a restaurant!

RICHARD:
But—raw—

LOUIS: I'm having trouble getting you.
Did you say "raw"?

DE COIGNY: He did.

MARIE: Disgusting!

LOUIS:
(*To* SERVANT)

                                        Do
Exactly as he says. Bring uncooked squid—
Lots of it.

SERVANT: But the chef won't—

LOUIS: I forbid
The chef to sear it even slightly. Raw!

(*The* SERVANT *scuttles away.*)

DE COIGNY:
(*To* MARIE, *quietly*)
I've got another squid for him to gnaw.

LOUIS:
(*To* RICHARD.)
You'll be yourself in just a little bit.
Can you talk more? What was it like?

RICHARD:
(*Reacting with pain*)

                                The hit!

LOUIS:
Those giant teeth! I thought you'd be more bruised.

RICHARD:
Not teeth. The metal claw.

MARIE: Oh, he's confused.

RICHARD:
(Touching his back)
It hit me here. I tried to get away.

LOUIS:
No, you were swallowed, eaten—

RICHARD: Couldn't stay
Above, but when I tried to go below,
The claw, it pulled me up, I couldn't go.
I turned up to the light, the clumsy fish
Was floating on the top. Why would they wish
To kill me, all these tiny creatures there?
But I can kill them first, if they won't spare
My life. I swam up underneath, my jaws
Agape. Kill or be killed, the moral laws
Agree. I bit. The floating fish collapsed.
The tiny beings scattered. Time elapsed
So quickly. I must smash them one by one,
Or they will stab me more—I've seen it done.
My tail a weapon, crushing one of them.
But then, a sound, a weakling cough of phlegm
Drew my attention. Here before me bobbed
One of these creatures, then he quickly lobbed
Another claw at me. I had no choice—
I ate him. But that did not still his voice!
I heard barbaric noises in my gut,
Distracting me. I tried to flee them, but
A third claw jabbed into my skin! Then more!
Now plunging deeper, faster than before!

*(RICHARD collapses, and makes the biggest moan/booms he's
made yet. The others stare at him, then at each other for a
moment. Finally LOUIS goes to comfort RICHARD.)*

LOUIS:
Oh, please don't relapse to those sounds again!
We much prefer you speak the speech of men.

MARIE:
What can these strange disordered words portend?

DE COIGNY:
He's lost his mind! Who wouldn't?

LOUIS: I'll defend
His honor. Don't you understand? He is
The fish. The fish is him. Its soul is his.
Its body died while he was deep within,
In essence he was part of it, begin-
-Ning the digestive process. Now where could
That lost soul flee but into him? This good
And honest man who said he's born to sail
Has got his wish—he's turned into a whale!

MARIE:
That's far-fetched, dear.

LOUIS: But you have seen—

DE COIGNY: A fit
Of great proportion—

MARIE: Nothing more.

LOUIS: Bullshit!
We've evidence! His words are perfect proof!

MARIE:
They're only words.

DE COIGNY: Or lies.

LOUIS: Shut up, you pouf!
If he's deceiving us, why would he then?

DE COIGNY:
The King called me a pouf!

MARIE: The hearts of men
Are full of unknown motivations—

LOUIS: Yes,
But he does not care what we think.

MARIE: I guess.
But is there still a man in there? Knock, knock!
(*Knocks on* RICHARD's *head.*)

LOUIS:
Marie, that's disrespectful!

MARIE: Poppycock!
If he's a whale, he's nought but oil to us.

DE COIGNY:
And we make candles of his sex.

LOUIS: Discuss
This at your leisure. He's a man to me.
A whale as well. He's what he wants to be.
Now, Richard, or can we still call you that?
Are you a man or whale? One caveat:
It is the King who gives you this exam—
You must not fail, lad.

RICHARD: I am that I am.

MARIE:
That's ominous.

DE COIGNY: No shrinking violet there!
So now he speaks for God—

LOUIS: He has a flair
For prophecy. Of course! Tiresias
Was blind, Cassandra mad! He's come to us
With words of wisdom no one understands.

MARIE:
Let's quiz him on the news of other lands.
America—how goes it there?

RICHARD: It's free.

(*The* SERVANT *returns with the raw squid.*)

LOUIS:
You see, he's kept his human memory.
Ah, here at last—the promised nourishment.

SERVANT:
The squid. Uncooked.

(As it is placed before him, RICHARD, starts gorging on the squid with an appetite like, well, a whale. The SERVANT whispers in LOUIS' ear.)

LOUIS: Eat to your heart's content.
I must be off. It seems I'm very late
To sign a law or some affair of state.
De Coigny, please attend to me. Marie,
Can you see to our present company?

MARIE:
(Watching RICHARD scarf the squid)
Of course, my dear. Though I anticipate
A conversation lacking in debate.

LOUIS:
His words are few, but oh so very wise.
Be kind to this God sent us in disguise.

(DE COIGNY and LOUIS leave. RICHARD continues eating.)

MARIE:
All right, he's gone.

(RICHARD keeps eating.)

MARIE: Please stop—I'm getting sick.

(RICHARD continues eating.)

MARIE:
Catch me—I'm faint!
(Swoons)

RICHARD:
(Throwing the remaining squid to the floor, catching her.)
                     You never miss a trick!

MARIE:
You're getting smelly squid all on my dress.

RICHARD:
Then take it off.

MARIE: That's to the point, I guess!
When you're a man, you are a man. You pounce!

RICHARD:
You'll find I'm still a whale where it counts.

MARIE:
Despite reports, I'm faithful to my King.

RICHARD:
Then stay that way. You needn't do a thing.

(RICHARD's *hand goes in* MARIE's *dress. She reacts.*)

MARIE:
Hands off! I said I love my Louis—

RICHARD: —But
He's not the man you crave—

MARIE: Stop talking smut!
I've servants everywhere. You're too risque.

RICHARD:
But I'm your servant, too, and want my pay.

(RICHARD *kisses* MARIE. *She struggles, but not much.*
Lights fade on them. Lights up on DE COIGNY *and* LOUIS *in*
a separate space.)

LOUIS:
His progress is encouraging, each hour
He's stronger, uses longer words. The power
Of his cogitation has increased—
The mind of man, the energy of beast!

DE COIGNY:
Still eating only squid?

LOUIS: He's gone through rooms
Of squid! Astonishing, what he consumes!

DE COIGNY:
Still spouting silly democratic rant—

LOUIS:
He's an American, you know. He can't
Help that. Religious freedom is a theme
As well. He's got an interesting scheme
For legally decreeing throughout France
The sacred rights of Jews and Protestants.

DE COIGNY:
You're listening?

LOUIS: Of course, I am amused
By much of what he says. But I have used
A quote or two among my cabinet
To great effect. His words are weird, and yet,
That's typical of prophets—not believed
Till it's too late. I have not been deceived,
But hear an underlying honesty
Contrasting with the court's vain flattery.

RICHARD:
(Appearing)
This week I've made a study of the laws
That fuel the revolutionary cause.
At risk of sounding slightly negative,
I think your tax reforms are tentative
Or one might even say irresolute.

DE COIGNY:
No, flattery is not his strongest suit.

LOUIS:
You're like a sibyl here on premises
To point this out.
(To DE COIGNY)
                    He tells it like it is.

DE COIGNY:
It's not as if you've not heard this before.

LOUIS:
But his perspective's too fresh to ignore.

RICHARD:
My people suffered revolution, too.

LOUIS:
America fought England, overthrew
An empire overseas. Our discontent
Is knocking at my door.

RICHARD: I represent
Another race as well.

LOUIS: The whales, you mean?
Then tell me of your people submarine.

RICHARD:
You've only seen us floating in the sea
Or processed into oil or wax. But we
Were once so much like you.

LOUIS: You walked on land?

RICHARD:
We breathe your air today. Give me your hand.

(LOUIS *gives* RICHARD *his hand.*)

RICHARD:
Five fingers here, composed of blood and bone.
A whale's fin has fingers, too, not flesh alone.
And there are five, just like a man's, like yours.
Where you have legs, a whale is smooth, but scores
Of tiny bones are hidden in his side,
The remnants of a strong and sturdy stride.

LOUIS:
That whales may once have walked, I don't dispute,
But why and how'd they fall in disrepute
And lose the privilege to roam the earth?

RICHARD:
I wonder what that privilege is worth,

When terra firma's thrice outpaced by wet,
And you can only sail the surface yet.

LOUIS:
So you're content to live in murky brine?

DE COIGNY:
And eat raw squid—

RICHARD: It's far too late to whine.
But when we lived on land we ruled it all,
So sometimes it's nostalgic to recall
The splendors of our royal race.

LOUIS: Such as?

RICHARD:
The rocky island you call England has
A plain on which we built a calendar
To mark the days. A simple cylinder
Of stone that heeds the sun.

LOUIS: That's Stonehenge, then!

RICHARD:
The pyramids are ours.

LOUIS: It's said that men
Could never have the strength to move those stones.

RICHARD:
We were a race of giants and our bones
Are often found today deep underground.
Unluckily we still remained Earthbound.
We conquered all the land, the sea, the air.
Were masters of our universe, and there
Were none upon the planet to contest
My race. It took a higher force to wrest
Us from our arrogant and happy place.

LOUIS:
That's God, you mean!

RICHARD: If God lives in the space
Beyond the planets and the sun, you may
Be right. The legend is that one bright day
Our capital, an island paradise,
Paid for our sins and made the sacrifice—

LOUIS:
What sins?

RICHARD: I'm too ashamed to say out loud.
This city was a glory crowned in cloud—
The architecture far outshone Versailles—

LOUIS:
Impossible!

RICHARD: We didn't even try.
For man was nothing in that gorgeous time,
Beneath the notice of our paradigm.
Too small, too weak, and not so very bright,
Not worth a single thought, much less a fight.
But look how you have prospered in our loss,
When all our great achievements turned to dross.

LOUIS:
What was the sacrifice?! Did they all drown?

RICHARD:
We still don't know for sure what brought us down.
A judgment fell from heaven, balls of flame,
That sank our city and destroyed our fame.
The sea embraced my people as its own,
We lost our legs, our fingers, and have grown
Into the creatures known as whales today
Who fuel your lamps and light your way.

LOUIS:
Atlantis!

RICHARD: What?

LOUIS: The city's name—I'm sure!
A continent that sank into obscure
And almost nameless darkness in the sea.

RICHARD:
You humans may have named our apogee
Millennia beyond our golden age.

DE COIGNY:
Now, let me understand you, Monsieur Sage:
Atlantis, Stonehenge and the pyramids
Built by Gargantuas who hit the skids
And then degenerated into whales?

LOUIS:
That's what he said!

DE COIGNY: I guess the Holy Grail's
Theirs as well, and ancient Pompeii, too.

LOUIS:
De Coigny, you're a cynic and a shrew.
These monuments concealed in mystery
Have been revealed now by this history.
His tale explains so much!

DE COIGNY: Oh, I attest
To that! Too much, I think. Might I suggest
That we recall the author of this tale
Has had his soul coopted by a whale—

LOUIS:
We live in extraordinary times—

DE COIGNY:
And witness extraordinary crimes
Like this absurd and silly blasphemy.

RICHARD:
I'm not at all concerned that you believe,
But if the King does not, then I will grieve
For France as for my dead ancestral home.

How tragic if the French should have to roam
Like whales?

LOUIS: Or Jews!

RICHARD: —Because God's wrath
Fell on your capital as well. I see your path
Is leading there. Your sins, like ours, to feast
While others starve—

DE COIGNY:
This thing—half man, half beast—
If we believe that this possession's true—
Is not a creature to be listened to!

RICHARD:
The arrogance of man! The pious scorn!
Assuming you're the highest creature born!
You call yourselves in God's own image made,
But every species sees its glories fade
And you're just this year's fashion. I've been sent
To warn you of your peril. My descent
Into this feeble flesh from nobler birth—
Your savior now incarnate here on earth!

(DE COIGNY and LOUIS and stare in shock as the lights fade
on them and come up on MARIE, wearing a cloak, once again
talking with a seated LOUISE in her cell. MARIE carries a
box. A portable bathtub is between them.)

MARIE:
Madame, I don't have time for pleasantry—

LOUISE:
That's good, because you're getting none from me.
It's time to have my therapeutic bath,
You're rushed—I won't deter you from your path.

MARIE:
I've brought a gift, a crèche from Portugal.

LOUISE:
(Reluctantly accepting the box)
A bribe, you mean.

MARIE: It's undeniable.

LOUISE:
(Taking out figurines)
Religious, too. How you manipulate!

MARIE:
You do collect ceramics?

LOUISE: As of late.
Because they're made of clay and so are we,
They bring to mind our own fragility.
(Breaks a figurine)

MARIE:
You've just destroyed the Mother of our Lord!

LOUISE:
Your namesake, is she not?

MARIE: You can't afford
To flout me so.

LOUISE:
In this "enlightened" time
All France is flouting God. I'm old. My crime
Is judged by Him, and so are you. Oh, look!
The three Wise Men—according to the Book
They also came with gifts of gold and myrrh
and frankincense. I don't suppose you were
The sort of girl who learned what each gift meant?

MARIE:
Oh, I forget.

LOUISE: Well, then, with your consent—

(MARIE nods.)

LOUISE:
The frankincense for worshiping a god.

And gold to pave the path a king has trod.
But myrrh embalms the body of a man.

MARIE:
Oh, I remember now—I think I can—

LOUISE:
They represent—

MARIE: The natures of the Christ—
God, king, and man.

LOUISE: The pearl highly priced.

(As they both smile:)

MARIE:
Our paths converge from time to time, Madame.

LOUISE:
Oh, look! How cute! A perfect little lamb!

MARIE:
You are devoted to the monarchy?

LOUISE:
With all my soul. And God, of course.

MARIE: *Mais, oui!*
If you could save the *ancien regime,*
Would you consider that *succes d'estime?*

LOUISE:
But how could I, a nun encloistered here?

MARIE:
Oh, stop! Your tentacles reach far and near.
Did I say tentacles? No, influence
Is what I meant.

LOUISE: I'm serving God—

MARIE: And France.
You shelter nuns who've run off, been abused,
With special succor so they won't look bruised
Or set upon by men.

LOUISE: My charity.

MARIE:
Your treatment—I'll avoid vulgarity—
Reduces swelling in their festering shame—

LOUISE:
I clean them up—God works his will. I claim
No power of my own. But miracles
Occur to those God loves and obstacles
Just melt away like rain. Why do you ask?

MARIE:
No fear, Madame—I won't take you to task,
Though some might say you work against God's will.

LOUISE:
I never—!

MARIE: Calm yourself, relax, be still.
What if I should offer you a chance
To save a girl, serve God, and render France
A service that might save the monarchy?

LOUISE:
We teeter on the verge of anarchy!

MARIE:
One tiny push—we fall in the abyss.

LOUISE:
What kind of push?

MARIE: Oh, something such as this.
(*She removes her cloak to reveal a small but obvious
pregnancy.*)

LOUISE:
I'll mince no words. I am your enemy.

MARIE:
Whom God instructs to love.

LOUISE: This cannot be
My nephew's doing.

MARIE: No, it's not. Else why
Would I resort to you?

LOUISE: Just blink an eye,
And I could have you ruined, arrested, killed!

MARIE:
But no one else in France is quite so skilled,
Or has a stake in monarchy. I fall,
And France falls with me, though I know they call—
—You call! —Marie a whore, this is the first
I've strayed from Louis' bed.

LOUISE: This is the worst
You could have done! But can't you simply say
The child belongs to Louis—

MARIE: There's no way
That that will work. The father and the King
Are many worlds apart. They're not a thing
Alike. I'm certain that it would be known.

LOUISE:
You reckless fool! You wait too long! You've grown
For what?

MARIE: —Five—

LOUISE: —Months! That's weeks too late—

MARIE:
I didn't say it was five months—just wait—

LOUISE:
I'm never wrong. You're five months gone. Delays
Like this can seal a girl's fate.

MARIE: Five days.

LOUISE:
I'd say, if suicide was not a mortal sin—
Five...days?

MARIE: That's right.

LOUISE: Impossible!

MARIE: I'm in
The fifth day of this pregnancy, but look
Five months along.

LOUISE: Then something's wrong—

MARIE: I took
Precautions, but this child insists on birth
And not in months, but days! My bursting girth
Bespeaks a vigorous and healthy sprig
Who's going to be—God save me!—rather big.

LOUISE:
I cannot save you from this monstrous child.

MARIE:
Oh, come on, now, you're hardly undefiled!
While you have this on me, I've more on you!
If either of us blabs, then both are through.
But I shall advertise, if you insist,
That you're the country's best abortionist.

(LOUISE *and* MARIE *glare at each other as the lights on them fade. Lights up on* LOUIS *and* RICHARD, *suspended, swimming.*)

RICHARD:
In water we are born, and to it shall return.

LOUIS:
That's true for whales—for men it's dust.

RICHARD: You yearn
To swim again in waters of the womb,
But at your death lie in a cold, dry tomb.
While he who dies encradled in the sea,
Is born again at once, quite instantly.
In oceans life is all connected—one.
This murder you call whaling has begun
To undermine that balance—life and death.

My people cannot surface, take a breath,
Without a harpoon sticking in our backs!

LOUIS:
Their deaths may yet save France with oil and wax—

RICHARD:
Already whaling ships seek southern climes
To find the cachalots in former times
Were feeding off your coasts and bred in bays
Of Spain and Portugal. But now those sprays
Of whales' deep exhales are rare up north—
My species seldom dares to venture forth.
I beg that you, the King of France, set down
A policy that shames the world around,
And bans the taking of sperm whales—

LOUIS:
I can't, unless our whaling venture fails—

RICHARD:
The economic woes of France have yet
To be addressed. You can reduce the debt
If you will spend more thoughtfully,
Instead of wasting cash on frippery.

LOUIS:
The people love the flash! I must uphold
The Sun King's standard, live a reign of gold—

RICHARD:
I don't see golden showers trickling down
Among your people.

LOUIS: When you wear a crown,
Your life's no longer yours, you're forced to romp
The public streets in circumstance and pomp.

RICHARD:
The Sun King's excess showed this continent
Exactly how its gold should not be spent.

And though a King for all modernity
He's not the greatest in eternity.

(Lights up on LOUISE *pouring hot water into a bathtub that contains* MARIE.*)*

LOUIS:
What king is greater than Louis Fourteen?
None living, that's for sure! None I have seen!
No kings of history, not Charlemagne,
Not Alexander, Caesar, Tamerlane,
Elizabeth of England, Genghis Khan,
A host of lesser monarchs, Solomon
And Russia's Peter (not so very great),
Frederick Barbarossa, Henry Eight?

RICHARD:
These aren't the kind of rulers that I mean.

LOUIS:
Who then, the Queen of Sheba? Constantine?

RICHARD:
Though other monarchs now are dead and gone,
This humble King's acclaim lives on and on.
He had no earthly treasure to amass.
His crown—of thorn, his steed a lowly ass.
His kingdom not of gain, but one of loss.
He carried not a scepter, but a cross.

(Irritated and bested, LOUIS *swims a little bit away from* RICHARD.*)*

MARIE:
Be careful, that's too hot! You're scalding me!

LOUISE:
To have the honey, one must brave the bee.

MARIE:
I have baths all the time. How will this help?

LOUISE:
(Still pouring)
If you start to blister, give a yelp.

(MARIE *gasps at the heat but endures.*)

RICHARD:
(Blindly swimming toward the petulant LOUIS)
I risk offending you each time I speak.

LOUIS:
Then hold your tongue a while, albino freak.

(They swim in silence.)

MARIE:
I've soaked here for an hour. I'm a prune!
If I stay any longer, I will swoon!

LOUISE:
The heat is penetrating deep within
To purify your shame and purge your sin.
I'll clean you in and out—

MARIE: I'm getting bored!

LOUISE:
—To make you ready to receive our Lord.

MARIE:
Hold on a moment! I'm not gonna die!

LOUISE:
Of course not!

MARIE: I'm a fool—God knows, you'd lie!
(Starts to get up)
That's quite enough.

LOUISE: Please, just a moment more!

MARIE:
(Clutching her belly and slipping back into the water)
What's this?

LOUISE: A pain—

MARIE: Yes, sharp! Please help!

LOUISE: You whore!
You're used to being coddled all the time,
But now you'll pay a price that fits your crime!

(MARIE *moans helplessly as* LOUISE *looks on. The lights on them dim.*)

LOUIS:
I owe you an apology. I'm scared
Of what the future holds. You dared
Suggest a model for a righteous king,
And though I know that's true, a little thing
Called crucifixion weighs upon my mind.
If that's your counsel, then I'm disinclined!

RICHARD:
But sacrifice is central to the theme
Of righteous governance. I might blaspheme
But Christ, to drag his children from the mud,
Has offered us his body and his—

(*Lights out instantly on* RICHARD *and* LOUIS *and up on* MARIE *and* LOUISE. MARIE *is still in the tub and* LOUISE *holds her hand.*)

MARIE:
(*A scream*)
                                      Blood!

LOUISE:
(*Looking into the tub*)
The evil's purging, that's how it begins!
Praise God! You'll soon be free of sins!

MARIE:
It won't let go!

LOUISE: It's coming.

MARIE: No, it's not!

LOUISE:
Be patient—you've already passed a clot.

MARIE:
This child?

LOUISE: It's not a child yet!

MARIE: —Though torn
From in my womb, insists on being born
In its own time, and now's too soon.

LOUISE: Just try!
It's starting to poke forth.

MARIE: I'm gonna die!
Please pull it out!

LOUISE: I can't. My hands are clean.
I've only given you a bath.

MARIE: I'm queen—
And order you on pain of death to pull!

LOUISE:
It happens on its own!

MARIE: You're pitiful!
I'm not miscarrying—I've been induced!
You've killed this child—

LOUISE: I've not!

MARIE: —Just like you've loosed
A thousand other babes from bonds of life!

LOUISE:
They usually rush to heaven, free from strife
Of living—

MARIE: This one won't! It wants to live!

LOUISE:
It does seem stuck—

MARIE: It is!

LOUISE:
(Positioning herself to pull)

May God forgive—!

(LOUISE pulls. MARIE shrieks and passes out. LOUISE falls back, her hands covered with blood. Silence for a moment as LOUISE sees her bloody hands. She gets up and goes to MARIE.)

LOUISE:
Your Majesty— Marie— It's out at last.
I'll clean you up. Our thanks to God that's past.

(LOUISE glances into the tub and is puzzled by what she sees. She peers more closely, then puts her hand to her mouth to stifle a scream that won't come. Lights fade on LOUISE and MARIE and come up on LOUIS and RICHARD, still swimming.)

RICHARD:
Start small with sacrifice: The King agrees
To let his people worship as they please.
Their troubles are impossible to stem
But you, at least, no longer feast on them.

LOUIS:
I don't devour my subjects! Don't say that!

RICHARD:
They sweat your daily bread. You're getting fat.

LOUIS:
This theme—you make it sound so literal.
It's just a metaphor—

RICHARD: Unnatural
To eat one's children, everyone agrees.
Infanticides and cannibals—of these
Which is the worst? To eat your young combines
These heinous sins, which means the one who dines
On his own child must be cast down, destroyed,
His power, however great, is null and void—

LOUIS:
I wonder if your passion for this sin
Relates to your own people's origin.
You intimated some disgusting deed
Caused God to cast them down and make them feed
On squid and slime in fitting punishment.
Your giant race, did they take nourishment
From their own children?

RICHARD: Yes, it did occur.

LOUIS:
Aha! Then I know who your people were!

(Lights fade on LOUIS *and* RICHARD *and come up on* DE
COIGNY, MARIE, *and* LOUISE, *who's now in bed.* MARIE
looks fine.)

DE COIGNY:
Madame, your nephew sends you his regrets,
And asks the Queen to don her briolettes
Then rush home to Versailles.

LOUISE:
(Reaching out, blindly)
                        What's that? Who's there?
Is that a man I hear? What man would dare?

MARIE:
She's been delirious for days.
(To LOUISE*)*
                        You're ill,
Madame. And though you're safely cloistered still
The strictest rules have been relaxed for you.

LOUISE:
That can't be right!

DE COIGNY: I'm from the King. It's true.
The Duc de Coigny come to take the Queen.

LOUISE:
(Seizing his hand)

The Duc! At last you've come! What I have seen!
So much to tell!

MARIE: She thinks you're d'Orleans.

DE COIGNY:
(*Loudly, to* LOUISE)
The Duc de Coigny—

LOUISE: Yes, my dear! Eons
Have passed since you've been here. That girl,
Your cousin's whore—

DE COIGNY: See here!

MARIE: Not for the world
Would I prevent her speaking now! Let's hear!

LOUISE:
She's turned out worse than I could ever fear!
Remember—on her very day of birth
Great Lisbon fell when God's wrath smote the earth.
A horrid clap of thunder rent the sky
The moment that she set foot at Versailles.
As if these omens weren't enough to heed,
A hundred people died in a stampede
The day she married Louis. He's so dim
He can't see how she's tricked and tainted him,
Bewitched his little brain, so he might call
A meeting of the Estates General.
But if he does, you must give quick assent
Then use it—seize the reins of government
Before he grants religious liberty
To Protestants whose heinous heresy
Will be the end of France!

DE COIGNY: Too late, Madame.

MARIE:
He's done it?

DE COIGNY: Yesterday he signed—

LOUISE: I am
Not well enough to hear this news—I'm sick
To death. To paradise, full gallop—quick!

MARIE:
And now you are her coachman, too. Farewell,
Madame.

LOUISE:
(Grabbing her hand)
                    Oh, Sister, one sweet drop of that prunelle.

DE COIGNY:
(To MARIE as she gives LOUISE a tiny glass of liqueur)
And who are you?

*(MARIE cautions DE COIGNY silence with a finger to her
lips.)*

LOUISE: You've been so kind.

MARIE:
(Kissing LOUISE's forehead)
                                                  Adieu.
You hate me, but you've been kind to me, too.
(She leaves.)

LOUISE:
Lean in, I'll whisper of that Antoinette
A tale that's got to be the worst thing yet!

*(Lights dim on LOUISE and DE COIGNY as he leans in and
she whispers in his ear. Lights up on MARIE and LOUIS.)*

MARIE:
What news so vital summons me away
From Auntie's deathbed?

LOUIS: Louise died today—

MARIE:
I missed that part—the end of all her sneers:
A moment I'd been waiting for for years.

LOUIS:
I know you loathed each other, even so,
She once was good.

MARIE: In ways you'll never know.
What news? Our Richard's well, I hope?

LOUIS: I've made
A study of this man's last gasconade
About his ancestors the giants who
Built Stonehenge, pyramids and Timbuktu.
Remember how he said a sin had drawn
God's fierce and fiery anger down upon
His kind?

MARIE:
          Oh, yes, and changed them into fish.

LOUIS:
Now I've deciphered all that gibberish.
He's chided me while you were gone about
Us eating peasant brats like so much trout.
He kept it up and said there's nothing worse—

MARIE:
I must agree.

LOUIS: Why something so perverse?
Because that was his people's sin—my final clue.
His people were the Titans.

MARIE: No!

LOUIS: It's true!
At least it makes a lot of sense. A race
Of giants used their kids for bouillabaisse.
Remember in Greek myth how Cronus feared
A deadly prophecy and engineered
To eat his children soon as they were born—

MARIE:
Oh, hon, I didn't read that stuff.

LOUIS: The warn-
-Ing wasn't heeded, or was heeded wrong,
And Zeus was hidden, nurtured until strong
Enough to cast his father down.

MARIE: That's all?
A lot of theory based on facts so small.

LOUIS:
There's more. He said Atlantis was theirs, too.
And who's Atlantis named for?

MARIE: Don't know. Who?

LOUIS:
It's Atlas!

MARIE: So?

LOUIS: He was a Titan!

MARIE: Oh.
(Sees DE COIGNY, *signals him over*)
Thank God you're here! My husband's turned Pierrot
And clowns with me about that whaler's pedigree.
He says he comes from Titans.

DE COIGNY: I can see
That now you bring it up. His current state?
It seems our Richard's gained a little weight.

LOUIS:
I meant to say—he's turned quite rubbery—
More to the point, he's big and blubbery.

MARIE:
Now, gentlemen, you're ribbing me!

LOUIS: He's huge!

DE COIGNY:
He's fat and gross!

MARIE: Don't take me for a stooge!
He's eaten too much—

LOUIS: Squid!

MARIE: That's all.

DE COIGNY: What parts
Of him are whale, what parts are man? It starts
To sound intriguing.

MARIE: Oh, you're bad.

LOUIS: My point
Is that his warning's not so out of joint.
We're living off our peasants' labor, not
Quite eating them alive, but here's a thought:
If we reduce expenses, trim the debt,
We might prevent a revolution yet.
The King's example leads nobility,
So I've cut down on costs. First Equerry?

DE COIGNY:
Your Majesty?

LOUIS: Your job at court is gone.
You'll have to earn your living from now on.

MARIE:
But Louis, that's not fair!

LOUIS: He's not alone.
I've fired your dressmaker as well.

MARIE: You've thrown
Them out while I was not at court?

LOUIS: That's right.
They're gone. You've come back home too late to fight.

DE COIGNY:
This whaler's wacky schemes have gone too far!

LOUIS:
It hurts when it hits home right where you are.
But don't despair. Don't look so woebegone.
Go find employment with Duc d'Orleans.
(*He leaves, smiling smugly.*)

DE COIGNY:
There's proof! He's never really liked me much.
But you can talk him out of it?

MARIE: Don't clutch
At straws. He's right. We've grossly overspent.

DE COIGNY:
But I'm reliant on emolument!
Your little plot has run amok with weeds!
The whaler's planted far too many seeds!
I've only you to blame for banishment,
Elaborate plans to fake a man's descent
Into the bowels of a whale, then pop
Him out to prophesy. But how to stop
His blatherings? Now what's your plan for that?
What other clever scheme have you begat?
You bleach and shave and pluck this pale boy,
Unleash him on the world, a deadly toy?

MARIE:
I'll not take credit—you're the mastermind,
The modest genius! Only you could find
A whale's stomach just when needed, hide
The poor, persuaded whaler deep inside—

DE COIGNY:
Oh, no—you taught him how to make that noise—

MARIE:
But you did that—

DE COIGNY: I didn't!

MARIE: No?

DE COIGNY: These ploys—

MARIE:
Weren't yours or mine!—

DE COIGNY: Another of your jokes?

MARIE:
The swallowing was real, not a hoax!

DE COIGNY:
Impossible!

MARIE: An accident, not planned,
And so much more effective. Understand?

DE COIGNY:
But didn't you confer with him before?

MARIE:
I planned for him to disappear—no more.
And then appear to Louis as a ghost.
The whale intervened and was his host,
Digesting him while dying. Yes, it's true.
Believe me, I'm as mystified as you.

(*Lights down on a stunned* DE COIGNY *and* MARIE. *Lights up on* LOUIS *guiding a very bloated* RICHARD. *They walk in silence for a moment, then suddenly* RICHARD *exhales violently through his mouth, spouting a fair amount of water into the air.*)

RICHARD:
How long?

LOUIS: Oh, twenty minutes. I'm impressed!

RICHARD:
I'm aiming for an hour.

LOUIS: That's quite a test.
Now, you were saying—Estates General?

RICHARD:
Convene them now and hold them in your thrall.

LOUIS:
They're not in thrall to me! The nobles shoot
Down all my laws—the clergy follows suit.

RICHARD:
The bourgeoisie and peasants love the crown.

LOUIS:
The peasants, yes—the bourgeoisie can drown!

RICHARD:
If you allot a double measure for
The Third Estate, nobility no more
Shall suck the blood of France. A giant tick
Will perish like you've smashed it with a brick.
The people will rejoice at liberty,
Equality, and yes, fraternity.

LOUIS:
I wish I could believe your prophecy.

RICHARD:
Then I shall prove it valid instantly.
(Groping blindly in his pocket)
Remember this?
(Pulls out a white taper)

LOUIS: The spermaceti oil
Made into candles, yes!

RICHARD:
(Pulling a bit of wax from the candle, giving it to LOUIS*)*
                    You humans spoil
Its properties. Here, warm it in your palm.
This substance is a myrrh-like kind of balm
That whales produce and carry in their heads.
When one of us is injured, then it spreads
Throughout the body, salving all the pain.
Has it turned soft?

LOUIS: I think so.

RICHARD: I'll explain
This while you demonstrate. Please daub my eyes.

*(*LOUIS *does so, gingerly.)*

RICHARD:
How old's a whale? He almost never dies
Unless harpooned by man. How can we live

Forever, never plagued by ills that give
You pain? Why, it's the spermaceti oil.

LOUIS:
A universal remedy?

RICHARD: We toil
Not, nor spin, and yet our raiment is
Eternity.
(Touches his eyes)
                   This heals the damages
Life does to us, if we are left alone,
But not if processed into oil and bone.

LOUIS:
So spermaceti oil is not your sperm?

RICHARD:
No truth in that, no, not a single germ.

LOUIS:
A pretty tale, but how to prove it's right?

RICHARD:
Well, how 'bout this? I've just regained my sight.

(LOUIS stares, then holds up his hand. RICHARD mimics the motion exactly. LOUIS holds up three fingers, and so does RICHARD.)

LOUIS:
It's true! You're cured!

RICHARD: You wasteful humans spurn
The wisdom of the whales. This balm, you burn.

LOUIS:
Astonishing!

RICHARD: Will this add credence to
My prophecy?

LOUIS: Yes, absolutely! You
Have won me over to the Third Estate!

(MARIE *appears.*)

LOUIS:
Marie! You won't believe it! This is great!
Our clever guest has had a wondrous thought
That when the Estates General meets we ought
To give the Third Estate their delegates
In equal number of the aggregates
Of clergy and the proud nobility!

(MARIE *just stares, cynically.*)

LOUIS:
And look! A holy marvel! He can see!

RICHARD:
The real miracle is what is seen:
My first sight is the gracious King and Queen.

MARIE:
(*Smiling tightly*)
Such wonders are so rarely manifest—
I'm glad to see it's worked out for the best.

LOUIS:
I called this man a prophet days ago
But underestimated him e'en so.
I realize, with what he's sacrificed,
He's less a prophet than a second Christ.

RICHARD:
But what if your conclusion is untrue?
Perhaps the role of Christ is saved for you.

LOUIS:
You told me sacrifice was in the cards.
Am I the sacrifice, then?

MARIE:
(*To no one in particular*)
                              Call the guards.

LOUIS:
My dear, his prophecies are tough but fair.

MARIE:
I see where this one's headed. What a pair!
You're Christ—am I the Virgin Mary then?

LOUIS:
Not quite. But you're a perfect Magdalen.

MARIE:
We're choosing roles as if this is a play!
It's not a tale—we're living it—today!

LOUIS:
We base our lives on fragments we recall
Of stories from our childhood. One and all,
We manufacture fictions into life,
For instance, like the one that you're my wife.

MARIE:
What's that supposed to mean?

LOUIS: It's been just fine
To keep the fiction that the Dauphin's mine.

MARIE:
He is your son!

RICHARD: Such rumors fly about
All heads of state these days. But there's no doubt
You can dispel all lies with one small act
Transcending gossip, fiction, fibs and fact.

LOUIS:
How wise he is! Marie, we must reveal
To all of France these truths—we can't conceal
This prophet, keep him to ourselves?

MARIE:
I'd just as soon confess to raising elves
At Trianon. I think you'd quickly find
The people saying that you'd lost your mind.

LOUIS:
I take advice from him because I must.
Sometimes he is the only one I trust.
(*Leaves in high dudgeon*)

MARIE:
Well? Satisfied? What have you done to him?

RICHARD:
Just what you asked.

MARIE: Destroy him on a whim?
He thinks he's the Messiah from your chat—
I think you know what always comes of that!

RICHARD:
Kill just one man? Not much ambition there.

MARIE:
How many are you catching in your snare?

RICHARD:
In pushing France into democracy
I'm giving each man power—

MARIE: That much I see.
But what's the harm? It's progress, isn't it?

RICHARD:
Perhaps it is. Perhaps the opposite.
The King has final say of life and death
For all his subjects, can cut off their breath.
The latest weaponry is his to use
To snuff them out as he may choose.
Imagine every woman, man, boy, girl
With power like that. It would destroy the world.
America and all its democrats
Are free to kill themselves like rabid rats.
And as for progress—moving on in life—
We strive for peace, but just engender strife,
And death-march ever closer to our goal—
Wrapped tightly in a sheet, dropped in a hole.

MARIE:
Your logic is intriguing, if macabre.

RICHARD:
That's fine. A sign that I have done my job.

MARIE:
A job for me! I gave you the King's ear!

RICHARD:
Oh, no, I took it for myself—that's clear!
You didn't help much.

MARIE: Impudence! I paid
You your full price.

RICHARD: Do you mean getting laid?
I took that, too. Remember who I am.

MARIE:
A man? A whale? I don't care where you swam—

RICHARD:
When I set sail for whale in search of God,
I'd no idea of the path I've trod
And was surprised as much as anyone to see
The God I sought at sea was really me.

MARIE:
Such arrogance! The Second Coming's you?

RICHARD:
This may not just be visit number two.
What if I've come before unrecognized?

MARIE:
We seek a god who's more idealized—

RICHARD:
The god within each man's a devil, too.
Titanic, angry, cruel. You'll have to face
Revenge: extinction of the human race.

MARIE:
I can't believe—if aught of this is true,
Then I'm at fault, for I created you!

RICHARD:
Aren't you at least amused by circumstance?
A whale brings down the monarchy of France.

MARIE:
The King is soft, but surely won't agree.
And you are out with just one word from me.

RICHARD:
The King won't hear you. No, he's hooked. He'll heed
My words. What paltry work to plant that seed!
I've done all that I need to make it stick.
(Touching her in an intimate way)
And, by the way, now you can call me Dick.

*(MARIE leaves quickly. Lights out on a smug RICHARD, and
up on DE COIGNY as he meets MARIE.)*

DE COIGNY:
He must be stabbed with lances. Let him die,
Then have his skin stripped off and liquefy
The fat to render oil. We'll drain his skull
Of spermaceti candle wax, then cull
His largest teeth and carve the ivory.

MARIE:
Not fond of him?

DE COIGNY: He's breeding anarchy!

MARIE:
And stole your place at court. It's personal.
The King's convened the Estates General
Just as we planned. It's only weeks away.

DE COIGNY:
But now we know he plans autos-da-fe
For all of humankind.

MARIE: I'm fond of him
And won't allow Dick killed.

DE COIGNY: The chance is slim
That he could be arrested, and the King
Would let him go. His plot could still take wing.
From respiration's labor set him free!

MARIE:
I'm sorry, no, he means too much to me.

DE COIGNY:
That's what I heard.

MARIE: The risk in that remark!
I am your friend, I thought you mine, you shark.
With words like that a life-long friendship dies.

DE COIGNY:
I tell the truth to save you from his lies!

MARIE:
That sounds a lot like blackmail to me.

DE COIGNY:
Just hear me out and I will guarantee
That you'll consent. What's more, the cornerstone
Of trapping him is when you meet alone
With him, out in the garden, late at night.
He must be done away with out of sight.

MARIE:
I've no intention to endorse your plot,
Whatever dirt you have on me, it's not
Enough to lead me to betray a friend.

DE COIGNY:
Perhaps, perhaps not—hear me to the end.
You will agree he must be killed.

MARIE: Not true.

DE COIGNY:
Madame Louise confided this—of you.

(Lights out on them and up on LOUISE.*)*

LOUISE:
I can't describe the thing within the tub
Except to say twas from Beelzebub.
The bloody mess so hideous and obscene—
To think that it had been inside the Queen.
Marie passed out and didn't see her spawn.
I scooped it up and ran across the lawn,
The dripping burden wrapped within a sheet.
No human eyes but mine would see that gleet
That issued forth from royalty. I thought
Of burying the sticky blob, but caught
Myself—someone could dig it up and trace
The evidence to Antoinette's disgrace.
The river wasn't far, so I climbed down
The moist and slippery rocks until the brown
And murky Seine was at my feet. I stood
There on the brink and wondered was it good
Or evil made me save the Queen, condemn
This thing I cannot call a child? But then
The strangest odor from my arms arose.
At first it was like fish that decompose,
But changed its strong aroma, smelled like lamb,
Delicious, roasted perfectly, a dram
Of mint—and then the horror of this meat
Reminded me that it was not to eat!
Revulsion seized my heart for this—decay—
I cast it off—and then it swam away!

(Lights out on LOUISE *and up on* RICHARD *in the garden.
Even though the lighting is dim, it's clear he's even more
bloated than before.)*

RICHARD:
De Coigny said she'd come, but looked so grim
I wonder if she'll give me any quim.

(Behind RICHARD, *in much dimmer light, a figure appears
wearing* MARIE's *cloak.* RICHARD *turns and sees the figure.)*

RICHARD:
Did you have second thoughts about this tryst?
(No response)
Perhaps you did, but needed to be kissed
So badly that you paid those thoughts no mind—
(No response)
You're here at any rate. I'm sure you'll find
You made the right decision.
(Touches the figure. It does not move.)
                                    Oh, we're cold
This evening, are we then? What if I told
A ghostly tale about a man who bet
That he could fool a king and minuet
In private with his queen?
(Stroking the figure in a more intimate way)
                                    An ancient tale,
Of course, repeated often, but a whale
Is part of this report, that much is new.
A magic myrrh now figures in it, too,
That heals all wounds, but not of man—
It only works on the cetacean clan.
This balm is one of three great gifts of old.
The second is an oil as rich as gold.
The third is ambergris of such expense
It's precious now as once was frankincense.
Wise men once gave these gifts unto their Lord.
We whales return them now as your reward.
You crave a man, De Coigny wants a king,
Poor Louis seeks a god—I'm everything!
(No response)
I was afraid you wouldn't come tonight.
For many days you've banished me from sight.
Though arrogant and bold, I know `tis true
That I will die without a word from you.

I pray you will acknowledge, if you can,
Your Majesty transformed a common man.
(No response. Reaches for the figure's crotch.)
Then tell me without words, for very soon—
What's this? You're not the Queen!

(The figure pulls a harpoon from within the cloak and presses the point to RICHARD's *throat. The figure pulls back the hood of the cloak, revealing that it is* DE COIGNY *crudely disguised as* MARIE.*)*

DE COIGNY: That's my harpoon
You're fondling, sir, and you shall have yours back.

RICHARD:
No need for that. I gave it up. Your knack
For switching loyalties has served you well.

DE COIGNY:
I'm loyal to myself, but I excel
At seeming what I'm not, I carry on
Not unlike you.

RICHARD: You serve Duc d'Orleans.

DE COIGNY:
He thinks I do. I seemed to serve the King
And acted like a loyal underling
Until today.

RICHARD: You shake. Are you afraid?

DE COIGNY:
It's righteous anger, for I've been betrayed.

RICHARD:
Betrayal's big tonight.

DE COIGNY: It's not.

RICHARD:
(Touching the harpoon at his throat)
                            What's this?
My lady, my harpoon—what's next, a kiss?

DE COIGNY:
This is your sentence for conspiracy.

RICHARD:
Same sentence for the ones conspired with me?

DE COIGNY:
You tricked us all, as you have just confessed.

RICHARD:
Not what I said. I might be truly blessed
With prophecy. I tell you now you won't
Crown d'Orleans the King of France. And don't
Imagine that the Estates General
Will help nobility to rise. Twill fall
As fast as monarchy comes tumbling down.

DE COIGNY:
Then who will rule France, if not the crown?

RICHARD:
My dire prediction is democracy:
The people rule, a form of anarchy.
When every man's a king, with power to kill,
They'll decimate themselves, and slay until
The human race is just a memory,
Or banished like the Titans to the sea.
My father spawned a revolution ere
He seeded me—now I exceed him there.

DE COIGNY:
What else do you predict?

RICHARD: I see your death.

DE COIGNY:
Then with those words you've uttered your last breath.

(DE COIGNY *harpoons* RICHARD. RICHARD *struggles
briefly, making whale sounds, then dies. As he is dying, two*
SERVANTS *isolated in light set a table.* MARIE *and* LOUIS
enter, seat themselves at the table and begin to eat. Lights

fade out completely on DE COIGNY *and* RICHARD *at the
moment of his death.)*

LOUIS:
I wonder would you help me with my speech?

MARIE:
Just as I always do.

(The SERVANTS *continue to add shiny banquet dishes to the
table, as well as white candles and oil lamps, until the table
is aglow with reflected light.)*

*(*MARIE *and* LOUIS *relish their feast.)*

LOUIS: I mustn't preach
At them, but win their confidence with kind
And gentle words.

MARIE: Be sure to keep in mind
Your goal of fairer taxes.

LOUIS: I don't care
So much about that any more.

MARIE: Don't scare
Me, darling.

LOUIS: But it's true. I've been alert-
-Ed by our Titan friend—

MARIE: We must avert
A revolution with the right reforms—

LOUIS:
Too late, my dear, we can't prevent the storms
From breaking out.

MARIE: But all your plans for free—?

LOUIS:
Your plans, Marie.

MARIE: Is this his prophecy?
That gloomy nonsense of apocalypse?

(DE COIGNY, *now dressed in his usual clothes, joins the*
SERVANTS *in serving food and adding lamps and candles to*
the table.)

LOUIS:
I promised not to say. Loose lips sink ships.

MARIE:
Our ship of state is sunk! You've been enticed,
Convinced yourself you play the role of Christ.
He's not a prophet, Louis—he's a man
Who told you all that stuff! It was my plan
To make you call the Estates General.

LOUIS:
Of course, I know, Marie. I know you all
Too well.

MARIE: But then you know that he's a fraud.

LOUIS:
(To a SERVANT)
Some more roast, please. It's good.

(SERVANT *gives* LOUIS *more meat. He eats it.*)

MARIE: His talk of God
Was prattle, all made up!

LOUIS: A pretty tale
Just the same. That bit about a whale
Descended from a Titan, very nice.

MARIE:
You mean you never fell for the device?

(DE COIGNY *squirts perfume with an atomizer.*)

LOUIS:
I feared it was a fiction from the start,
But liked the metaphor, and put my heart
Into the story, found the truth that hid
Inside the falsehood, little spermatid
Of great profundity. Just like we need

To drink the blood of Christ and humbly feed
On holy flesh—to transubstantiate—
I swallowed this new fiction—it was great.
The truth I found within was nothing new:
Our faith has power to make these tales true.

MARIE:
But Richard cannot be Jehovah's son—

LOUIS:
Or honest prophet—my faith made him one.
Consider this: when revolution rears
Its ugly head, the King will shed no tears
Though I'm convinced, my darling, you and I
Will be the sacrifice. We'll have to die.
But this is natural—how things progress.
Once God had all the pow'r, now kings oppress
The populace as if we were divine.
When they rise up and kill us, that's just fine.
It means the human race is winding down,
As other races disappeared—don't frown!
It makes a kind of sense—it's not so odd
With every man a king, therefore a god,
The race has reached perfection, climbed so high,
There's nowhere left to go—it's time to die.
Each sperm contains the seed of its demise—
The human seed its bloom and doom supplies.

MARIE:
Is that your speech?

LOUIS:
(Shakes his head)
                        They'd never understand.

MARIE:
Nor I! It's not too late. You must disband
The Estates General, rescind the call!

LOUIS:
Oh, no, my dear. It's not like that at all.

The seed that's planted cannot be unsown.
I'm giving up my power, my life, my throne.
Surprisingly, I'm not at all aggrieved.
I must confess, I'm mostly just relieved!
So let's relax, enjoy this lovely meal
And glorious candlelight.

MARIE: I think—

LOUIS: Just feel.
The time for rationality is past,
The Age of Reason's over, that was last
Year's fashion. Now indulge the senses for—

(DE COIGNY *sprays more scent.*)

LOUIS:
—You won't have use of them for long.

MARIE: Who wore
That scent—

LOUIS: Why, you did, dear. Gardenia, right?
I thought it apropos just for tonight.
It's out of season, but the scent is fixed
With ambergris. Now don't be shocked—I mixed
It up myself. I also helped to make
The candles and the oil. How's your steak?

(MARIE *suddenly stands up, trembling.*)

LOUIS:
Too tough? Perhaps too fishy for your taste?

(MARIE *just stares at* LOUIS.)

LOUIS:
Now, finish up. He mustn't go to waste.

(MARIE *doesn't move.*)

LOUIS:
I understand—you ate too much, might gag.
De Coigny, fetch my wife a doggie bag.

(DE COIGNY *puts* MARIE's *leftovers in a bag.* MARIE *is paralyzed with revulsion.*)

LOUIS:
It's nice to share Communion with one's spouse:
A King and Queen together in one house.
We haven't dined together since the Flood!
Especially on the Body and the Blood.

MARIE:
Louis, I loved you till this moment, but
However God may chastise, bruise or cut
You for your sins, how much it hurts—
I'll always say you got your just deserts.

LOUIS:
Marie, no good indulging in dismay—
He told me that he wanted it this way.

(DE COIGNY *hands* MARIE *the doggie bag. She faints. Nobody catches her. Lights out on the table as* LOUIS *moves to another area where he is isolated in light.*)

LOUIS:
(*Orating*)
I greet the clergy and nobility
My honest people and the bourgeoisie:
A heartfelt royal welcome to you all
As we convene the Estates General.

(*A happy cheer goes up from the crowd as the lights dim on* LOUIS *and come up on* MARIE *in her cloak, standing at the edge of the sea. She carries the doggie bag. Sounds of surf and sea birds*)

MARIE:
Do traitors die forgiven? I must know.
My death is imminent, and I have so
Betrayed a host of people in the space
Of months: my husband, lover, country, race—
Not to mention child, or progeny—

To speak with accurate phylogeny.
Perhaps, when you were thrown into the Seine
You floated to a mother more humane.
Like Moses in the Nile, a refugee,
You found the greatest matriarch—the sea!—
Who nurtures you for your revenge on Man.
But please forgive your mother if you can.
Another child that that same union bore
Still lives today and will forevermore—
The revolution's come, for what it's worth,
And I'm the wicked mother gave it birth.
A woman so completely stained by sin,
I can't imagine washing clean again.
If only I could know that you're alive
And see what you've become, and if you thrive.
I offer this, the ashes of your sire—
(Scatters ashes from the doggie bag in the sea.)
Our link from God to Man and my desire,
To lure you back to me and to the shore,
So I can see my—progeny—once more.

(Sound of a whale spout. MARIE *peers out to sea.)*

MARIE:
A veil of spray the answer to my prayer—
Come closer, where the water meets the air
And rocky shore falls off to deepest bay.
I see you there beneath the water gray.
I'm of dry land, and you of salty sea—
This moment we're as close as we will be.
Break through the surface, let me look at you—
(Splashing sound of whale surfacing.)
Magnificent! So like your father, too!
There's aught of me I see—a certain style,
However, gives you royal grace that I'll
Assume is my maternal legacy.
You help me to regain virginity
Of spirit when I gaze at you. Almost—

I see your father, pale as a ghost.
There's joy and terror in the shocking sight:
A whale of the purest, shining white.

(Lights dim slightly on the doting MARIE *and up on* LOUIS
in the midst of his speech.)

LOUIS:
You are my people, and my children, too.
And all my actions on behalf of you—

(Some whistles and catcalls)

LOUIS:
Are calculated—do not ask me how—
In your best interests—moving forward now—

(More catcalls. Lights dim on LOUIS *and up on* MARIE.*)*

MARIE:
If only there was some way you could sign
Forgiveness and acknowledge you are mine.

(A plume of spray shoots up as the whale spouts, soaking
MARIE. *She revels in her baptism.)*

MARIE:
Then only as your mother can I boast,
Invoke the Father, Son and Holy Ghost.
So wash me clean enough for paradise,
Prepare me for the coming sacrifice!

*(*MARIE*'s shower continues, and she glories in it. Lights do*
not dim on MARIE *but also rise on* LOUIS.*)*

LOUIS:
The future's here—I'm proud to play a part
I've studied all my life, with all my heart—

(Catcalls and grumblings increase, along with some
indistinguishable shouts. Some strange clicks and wheezes as
well.)

LOUIS:
You may not love me now, but you will see
How vital to this process I will be.

(Shouts grow louder and more incoherent, threatening to drown out LOUIS' words. The clicks and wheezes sound strangely familiar.)

LOUIS:
And sacrifice has got to play a role
In progress, giving up the strict control—

(The shouting has become a roar that almost completely obscures LOUIS' speech.)

LOUIS:
—Each human being wishes in his life.
I bow to your desires, and my wife
Will do the same. We care for you, you see,
Will only rest when all of France is free!

(LOUIS can no longer be heard, but continues to speak inaudibly as the roar grows in intensity and changes its character, sounding more and more like the whale booms RICHARD made. MARIE continues to welcome the repeated sprays of the whale's spout. The boom is now recognizably the whale sound, but louder and more intense than before. Finally it is so loud it sounds almost like a massive explosion. Lights quickly brighten everywhere then go out.)

END OF PLAY

www.ingramcontent.com/pod-product-compliance
Lightning Source LLC
Chambersburg PA
CBHW052117090426
42741CB00009B/1850